Beliefs, Boundaries & Balance

Tools To Finding Your
Way To Inner Peace

AUTHOR:

Jandy Kelley

authorHOUSE®

AuthorHouse™
1663 Liberty Drive
Bloomington, IN 47403
www.authorhouse.com
Phone: 1-800-839-8640

First published by AuthorHouse 3/28/2012

ISBN: 978-1-4520-1922-2 (e)
ISBN: 978-1-4520-1921-5 (sc)
ISBN: 978-1-4520-1920-8 (hc)

Library of Congress Control Number: 2010906347

Printed in the United States of America
Bloomington, Indiana

This book is printed on acid-free paper.

Table of Contents

Group Study Guide

This book is laid out to be both a self-read & guide and a group study. For group study, you may use the recommended methods below or choose your own preferred method. You will find this book/workbook is easy to navigate. Prior to starting your study, please read through the complete instructions for the path you have chosen so you will be readily prepared. Good luck!

3 Part Meeting- Once Monthly

Month 1-Before meeting:
Read & complete all of Chapter 1, Beliefs
Complete all end of chapter activities

At Meeting:
Have each participant discuss what negative internal beliefs they have discovered and how they are still affecting their life. Each participant will read 2-3 of their new positive beliefs that they have written about themselves. Open discussion on revelations & lessons achieved during this chapter.

Month 2-Before meeting:
Read & complete all of Chapter 2, Boundaries
Complete all end of chapter activities

At Meeting:
Have each participant discuss the unhealthy behaviors they have identified and are still executing. Detail how it holds them back and how they plan to make change. Participants will also discuss how they are not setting healthy boundaries in their lives and why and how they plan to make change.

Month 3-Before meeting:
Read & complete all of Chapter 3, Balance
Develop six-month self-development plan for post study group

At Meeting:
Have an open discussion on priorities & goals participants plan on achieving. Discuss other key activities that they plan on implementing to stay balanced. Discuss as a group the six month plans for staying on track with personal growth.

8 Week Study Meeting Once Monthly

Week 1-Before Meeting
Read Chapter 1

At Meeting:
Each participant will discuss which scenario best fits them from the twelve scenario's. Have the leader of the group read out loud the old negative belief list. Participants will make a check mark in their guide next to each negative belief that applies to them. Have open discussion about what individuals have discovered.

Homework: Have participants write all of their old negative beliefs into new positive beliefs. Have the participants bring them to the next meeting.

Week 2

At Meeting:
Open discussion about what individuals have gained in their understanding about negative beliefs and how they are holding them back. Participant will read 2-3 of their new positive beliefs to the group.

Homework:
- Write out verbal negative beliefs you received
- Write out behavioral negative beliefs you received
- Write the negative messages you are telling yourself
- Write the negative behaviors you are currently exhibiting

Week 3-Before Meeting
Read Chapter 2

At Meeting:
As a group, share and discuss the completed homework. Discuss the verbal negative beliefs participants received, the behavioral negative beliefs they received, the negative messages participants are telling themselves and the negative behaviors they are currently exhibiting. As a group, take the Oath of Peace & Happiness. Discuss the areas of communication they identified that they need to improve upon.

Homework: From Chapter 2, complete a "tree" for EACH negative belief.

Week 4

At Meeting:
Discuss the "tree activity" and what each participant discovered about how their negative belief and unexposed feeling is tying into their behavior and what it is holding them back from achieving.

Homework: Have participants Complete the Boundaries Inventory Graph.

Week 5

At Meeting:
As a group, discuss the Boundaries Inventory Graph. Allow each participant to share about their "non-accepting" behaviors that are holding them to the same outcomes.

Homework: Have participants identify and fill out how they do not set boundaries. Identify and fill out how they set too many boundaries. Write how they don't set boundaries and what they are giving away because of it.

Week 6

At Meeting:
Discuss boundaries as a group and how they are affecting each participant's life. As a team, build a "boundary charm bracelet" together. This will be a fun and bonding activity for the group and promote them to support one another in holding to their boundaries.

Homework: Have participants complete all the questions throughout each section of Chapter 3-behaviors. (ex. Fear, etc...) Please understand this may take more than a week. This is for each participant's continued self-development and will take time. These writing sections do not necessarily have to be discussed. If you choose as a group to review them, add 4 weeks to your study.

Week 7-Before Meeting
Read Chapter 3

At Meeting:
As a group, go through the priorities activity. As the leader, list out your priorities and then help others who may need assistance. Have each participant discuss how they have not lived in their priorities and how it has held them back.

In a group setting, begin laying out the goals participants want to achieve. From the goal topic list, each participant will make a page for each goal topic. They will begin writing out their personal short, medium and long term goals for each topic. Monitor the room for who may be needing assistance in completing this task.

Homework: Have participants purchase a poster board, a couple magazines, scissors and a glue stick (if they do not have). Bring these items to the last meeting.

Week 8-Before Meeting

At Meeting:

As a group activity, each participant will make their own vision board. This is a fun activity and promotes creativity. The vision board is to represent their life and work vision for themselves and their family. This is to include priorities and goals! Have FUN!

Disclaimer:

I will discuss many aspects of behavior and the impact our up-bringing had on us as children and how they can affect our adulthood. This book has been inspired through my own personal experience. I encourage you to find help and support through any means possible. These writings reflect my opinions and beliefs, and tools that helped me heal.

Please seek professional help if you feel that you are in need. The writer is not responsible for the actions of the reader and therefore the reader will not hold Jandy Kelley (or Labyrinth Coaching & Training, LLC) responsible for their actions due to the reader utilizing any of the information in this book. Jandy Kelley is not a licensed, certified or registered therapist, doctor or psychologist. Good luck with your journey.

SPECIAL THANKS TO:

GOD

PROLOGUE

I was broken. Trying to please everyone around me, I was weary in my spirit. I wasn't even sure if I had a spirit left. Or, did I ever really have one to begin with? I had become a people pleaser to such a degree that I sacrificed my body, my mind, my emotions, my relationship with God and well, okay...every other part of my life. Just name it.

I didn't even know who I was and I had not realized that most of the thoughts I had about myself or anything else weren't even mine. They were handed down like a tattered rag doll, wanting to be understood and loved as if new. The thoughts and beliefs I had didn't seem to line up with what I felt was right, deep inside of me. That was a part of me I had to squelch. If I didn't, I wouldn't survive. I surely wouldn't be accepted.

Acceptance... something that seemed far from my reach, yet I was willing to do anything to achieve this desired feeling. It was a dream, but a dream that didn't seem to be meant for me. So, I ventured to find it in any corner I could, destructive or not. Men would become something to conquer. There I surely felt that I would receive the love and acceptance I always wanted.

I became a human-doing. If I just DID more, someone would find value in me. Yes, I said it. I did not feel like I had value, that I was worthy or deserved acceptance. It wasn't just okay that I was born. I had to prove my worth; earn the right to be here. Even my own family made that clear. My sister told me when I was a teenager that she had resented me her whole life for my being born. Clearly, I was not smart enough to know I shouldn't have come here in the first place. There was no place for me.

So, I got busy. Busy doing! I felt like if I could just prove myself, I would achieve that golden dream. I would learn how to become the best people pleaser. I would learn to avoid my feelings. I would learn to be numb to knowing how to say, "No." I would get involved in things or situations or people where I was accepted, though the situation was clearly not healthy. At least I was wanted in that scenario. Better than nowhere.

I put my life at risk being with people I shouldn't be with; doing things I shouldn't be doing. I put my self-respect aside for a little glimpse of love. I did not understand how my behaviors would change the course of my life. I felt like God was going to have to do something fairly significant in my life to make this course change patterns, which He did, but that is another book.

The course: that is what it is all about. It is the beginning. The beginning of who we are. God brings us into this world lovingly by his grace, but not necessarily loved by the grace of anyone else. It is not that they don't mean too. Often times, it's that they don't know how to love, unconditionally and fully that is. The course of life is riddled with patterns that keep us in the state of being "human-doings", and keeps us out of the clutches of the "human being" model that is granted peace, love, acceptance and respect. It may even be that we are loved, but the patterns of negative behavior have such a strong-hold on the family, that it is by osmosis that you feel or act out failure.

No fault of yours you may be asking? Yes…and, no. How old are you? If you are past the age of eighteen, it is now officially your fault that you are swept up in negative beliefs, having no functioning boundaries in your life and a lack of peace that leaves you teetering off balance. Yet, at the same time, it is not your fault. How is one to know that they are not functioning well?

The symptoms are feeling stressed the majority of the time, saying yes when you want to say no and feel you cannot, pleasing people you don't even like or respect, allowing others to say or do things you do not agree with, making choices that you know are wrong, not taking time for yourself, not being financially responsible, loaning money when you don't have it, not setting boundaries and the list can go on.

This isn't about throwing your parents or caregivers, whom ever that may be, under the bus. It's not about that at all. It is about knowing what the real situation was and making it accountable to why you are here today with all of the many non-working behavioral ticks you may have. Accountability isn't about talking to your parents or caregivers about it. You have to become accountable first to yourself. Seldom does talking to the caregiver change anything. Change has to happen first with you.

I hated that fact...that change had to happen with me. Honestly, I was afraid. I was afraid to look under the hood of this dysfunctional mess and to admit how I got here. Even if you didn't come from a dysfunctional mess, you have to understand how you got to this very day, where you feel wired and tired and wondering how you are going to get to the next task, feeling like you have no peace in your life. It all starts with one thing...our beliefs.

There is a reason why you do not say no. It doesn't just happen by chance. Somewhere in our brain we begin to believe things. Whether positive or negative, these thoughts become our mechanism for our decision making. Often times these thoughts, that turn into beliefs, come from moments in our childhood that were influenced by our caregivers. Sometimes it is the people we choose to spend time with. Even teachers can influence our thoughts. Understand that thoughts have the power to become beliefs. It depends on your having a filter between them to decipher if they are healthy or not.

We are even taught to either have a filter or not. It makes sense that if our caregiver has a filter, we will likely learn to have one. If they do not, we likely will not. My family had no filters. My parents, being dysfunctional and alcoholics, made it impossible for me to have filters. Different family systems do not have filters for various reasons. It can come from alcoholism or any addiction, control issues, anger, abandonment, lack of boundaries, codependency and even mental disorders. For instance, a sociopathic person has no filters for feelings of others. It is literally a mental disorder. However, many filters are learned or not learned through your environment. Filters, put simply, are boundaries.

Boundaries were extremes for my family: either they were setting VERY strong boundaries that were unreasonable and mimicked walls or there were none to be had. This brought much confusion to my life and who I was. Signals were mixed and combined with a lack of filters which made for situations that left me to misjudge. For example; sitting at the dining table, I remember numerous times my mother telling me I could do anything I wanted as a career. But then there were times she would tell me stories of a friend of hers having been a stripper in the 1950s, and because of this, she was able to pay her way through college and become a lawyer. My mother then told me I would make a good stripper. But, of course, I could do anything I set my mind to. You can see the confusion that resulted from these twisted messages, as well as the inappropriate information that was not filtered by my mother or me.

Was she saying that I really couldn't do anything I set my mind to and so therefore I would have to use my body? Was she saying I wasn't smart enough to go to college? Was she saying that I wasn't worthy of her paying for college and I would have to pay my own way? Maybe this was her way of manipulating that point.

The key factor was that not only were these confusing verbal messages, but her behaviors backed it up. She never took me to the guidance counselor or took me to a college to learn how to enter school. That never happened. So, the behavior matched the message. It did not matter how many times she told me that I was capable of anything. The backup wasn't there.

So, it isn't a surprise that I came into my career at a much later date and through much heartache, lack of self-confidence and confusion. It is actually a miracle that I came into who I am and being successful at all. Many times subtle messages like this that we receive propel us into constantly proving ourselves. We become overworked, overstressed and do not honestly know how to be at peace. Because, the negative beliefs cause us to have inappropriate or nonexistent boundaries and without having boundaries, there isn't peace. You see, this is a DILEMMA! BTW, I never did become a stripper...I forget to share that bit of the story sometimes.

Chapter 1

Beliefs

*Guard your heart above all else for it determines
the course of your life. Avoid all perverse talk; stay
away from corrupt speech.* (Prov: 4 23-24)

You are:

Scenario #1

You have too many work meetings that run into late evenings. You are constantly juggling from one child's activity to another. You have church every Wednesday night and Sunday morning, as well as leadership involvement. You are married and have household duties to attend to, as well as family events with in-laws almost weekly. Your work is never done, and so you bring your work home with you, keeping you up at times into the wee hours.

Scenario #2

You have never really been alone. You went from home to a marriage or have always been in a relationship. You tend to be jealous and feel uneasy when you do not have others around. You get involved in your friends drama and tend to be the advice giver. You work very hard and over achieve in your job, yet feel empty inside. You have all of this going on, yet feel alone.

Scenario #3

You never say "no." Everyone loves you because you are so giving! People tend to think you are an angel because you are always there in a crisis. You volunteer at church and your local hospital. Your adult children often drop off their children with you at the last minute, but you are there for them in a pinch. You don't mention to your husband that you really do mind that he spends the weekends golfing with the boys even after not seeing him all week from work. Instead of taking much needed vacations you loan the money you have saved to your child who can't seem to keep a job and is still living at home. You KNOW though he has talent somewhere in there and one day will use it. You think the best of everyone and when disappointed think that it must have been something you did.

Scenario #4

You have always been admired for your beauty. No one thinks you have a care in the world. You walk strongly and confidently into a room. Friends talk about your jet-set lifestyle; if they only knew the debt that was behind it. Everyone thinks you have the best husband. You try to remember that when he is hitting you and you hide behind your sunglasses for days or don't leave the house. But, you are grateful to have the things that you have and your children need the stability of their father. This is what you tell yourself when you have those pangs of fear of leaving or of admitting that your life really isn't what is portrayed.

Scenario #5

School wasn't for you. That is for people who are privileged. You are street smart and proud of it. At least you don't have all those school loan payments. You know that you are a hard worker. You know your father always told you that you wouldn't amount to anything but you try not to think about that. You look around at your surroundings and think about how you wish you could win the lottery. Wouldn't that be a dream! Your boss tells you he doesn't know why you work in a menial job because you are very talented, but you laugh because he is the owner and you aren't worthy. Those kinds of opportunities are for other people.

Scenario #6

You work so hard all week and play just as hard. You don't shy away if a drink is handed to you. You don't see anything wrong with putting a few away at night after a long day. If it was okay for your parents it is okay for you. You know you should be better about getting up on time and not being late for work but feel that your boss shouldn't be so in your business as long as you get your work done. You don't know what the big deal is. It is hard for you to keep or make commitments when you said you would do something. People just need to understand you do things in your own time and that you don't like to be weighed down. You don't know why people get so frustrated or worked up when you forget details or conversations. Not having to think too much or hash out situations seems ideal to you...then you aren't disappointing anyone.

Scenario #7

You REALLY think THIS one is going to be the right guy! He won't be like the rest who have opened up very quickly too you, even proposing quickly and then disappearing. Well, even though he has opened pretty fast and is starting to talk about marriage, you see a difference in him. He wants a real commitment. Even though you have only been dating three months he wants to move in already, he must really love you to want to make a REAL commitment like that. You know that he is having some hard times having lost his job and being behind on some bills, but you know he is going to get that fixed because he said he is looking for a new job and once that happens, all of these problems will be gone. He told you so. You know paying the rent and utilities by yourself won't last long. You are so excited because in a few months, when all of this is handled, he said he wants to buy you a big engagement ring. He knows how you've always wanted a big diamond. It will look beautiful on your hand!

Scenario #8

You know your place as a good Christian girl is to not stir things up. Your mom and dad taught you so many wonderful and proper things in how to be a good young lady. You know your husband doesn't really mean it when he calls you those names. You avoid your feelings because once again you will just be a "drama queen" if you bring that stuff up. You know your friends really love you even though they seem to go away when they don't need something from you. You know at times they talk down to you but figure you deserve it. You know you don't make the best decisions at times and they are probably right.

Scenario #9

You know last night you should have just gone home instead of saying yes. Now you are trapped yet again. Hopefully he won't invite you to breakfast...that would just be painful. You said you would never do this again. You want to say no but when you are in the moment can't seem to. This is the third time the last few months that you have done this. Maybe you can get up and sneak out, just in time to go home and clean up so that you can go to church and make your parents proud. You don't want to disappoint them.

Scenario #10

You are the baby of the family. You know your parents love you, but you never seem to measure up. You make a good salary...but it isn't exactly what your siblings make. You make a lot of effort, even more than your siblings, but fault tends to find you first, even when not warranted. Comments towards you are not clear and you often feel guilty or like a failure. You just wonder why or how this happened. You think you are a good person, but don't know why you tend to be left out.

Scenario #11

You are always tired. Maybe it's because you are sick all the time. You know you should take better care of yourself. The doctor even said you really needed to lose 70 pounds. Exercise is just so hard and you are so busy. Well, at least during the day at work. But you are so tired when you get home. That couch just feels so good and you don't have time to really cook so the drive-thru is your friend. Next year, you will make it happen!

Scenario #12

You don't know what you feel. Is there even such a thing as feelings? You have long forgotten. It's just too much to remember. Who would want to remember all of that pain? You are just protecting yourself. Yes, that is it! If you don't feel anything then you won't have to admit what is boiling on the inside. I know people must wonder why you cry at the drop of a hat but then swear life is good. You have it all together!

Does one of these scenarios resonate with you? Do you recognize yourself to the point that you feel like I was standing outside your house and was writing specifically about you? Maybe you even see yourself in several of these scenarios. The issue is that it only takes one of these situations to know that we are not in a healthy state of mind, body or emotion.

This is where our lives become unbalanced and it is difficult, if not impossible, to ever reach a state of peace. Maybe you have a different scenario, but at the end of the day all of these situations boil down to the same feelings. Your story may not be like the person sitting next to you but that doesn't matter. Sadness is sadness. Anger is anger. Fear is fear. When we don't have peace in our lives, we have something else, something that may prove to be destructive to our goal of having inner peace.

What is peace anyway? It is something often talked about and often desired by many, yet few really grasp what it means or definitely what it feels like because they have never achieved it. For years now, here is how I have described peace. I see peace being a place that's achieved if you were to be locked in a dark room with no possessions, no loved ones, no clothes, NOTHING, and you would still be okay. In your mind, even though you would miss your loved ones and your possessions, you have so much self-love, esteem and a strong relationship with God, that you are internally happy. Of course you would have sadness and pain over your losses, but, you are okay. Sound impossible?

Look at particular prisoners of war who suffered for years being locked up in solitude with no possessions and no contact with the outside world. I remember seeing old footage of Senator, and once presidential hopeful, John McCain when he was held captive by North Vietnam. He spoke about how when he came into the war he was not exactly the most moral guy or particularly happy but more arrogant and self-centered. He went on to say how the years of solitude helped him to achieve an internal peace and resolve that changed him to the man he is now. This is only one account; I have seen others out there who talk about this occurring.

So, what does it take for the rest of us ordinary individuals to achieve peace without being detained in solitude? First and foremost, we have to have good beliefs about ourselves on board. If you fall into any of the twelve scenarios, I can pretty much guess that you may still have some negative beliefs about yourself. The reason why I say this is because when we feel good about ourselves, we make good decisions. When we feel good about ourselves, we stand up for ourselves. Not that someone who has positive beliefs about themselves can't make occasional mistakes or have situational issues of over doing, but, for the most part, their lives are well balanced. A person with negative self beliefs will tend to live in a chaotic cycle that tends to lean in the dysfunctional range.

Beliefs are deep seeded. They grow who we are. We are brought into this world by God and given a personality, but then we are directly influenced by those who raise us, usually our parents. We have to understand who is accountable for our behavior today. As previously stated, I'm not saying that you have to throw your parents under the bus. However, you do need to take an honest look at your life and distinguish exactly where you got your ideas, opinions and beliefs about life and yourself.

Many of my clients have a hard time making their parents or caregivers accountable. I explain that it is not about staying in the blame, but about knowledge. You see, you didn't sit down with a note pad at age 1, 4, 6 or 8 years old and begin creating a list of the things you are going to "sign up for" in life. At any point, did you decide that you wanted to be co-dependent, with low self-confidence, without boundaries, feeling worthless or any other negative feelings that you may be harboring? NO!

It is frustrating when I hear a client say, "I'm just this way, I'm just hard on myself." Most of the time, through further probing questions, the client will reveal a situation that put pressure on them to take on these issues.

Don't believe me? I love giving this homework to my clients. I tell them to go watch 2-3 episodes of a "popular" television show where two wives of two different families swap places for 2 weeks. It AMAZES me on that show how you will see two completely different families with two completely different value systems and the small children who will angrily defend the "family beliefs." These children will yell, cry and stomp off while arguing with an outsider adult. Where do you think they learned it?

Again, not to throw the parents under the bus, yet we need to have an honest understanding of where we learned things. It's not that our caregivers meant to give us a less than productive upbringing, yet it happens. It happens because they themselves were victims. They learned from their parents and then they pass it down. So, often times these issues are generational.

Take for instance, if your Great Grandma had been sexually assaulted. Your Great Grandma may have lived in the mid to late 1800s. During that period, situations like this were often hushed and the victim was told not to speak of it ever again. On top of that, the victim may have even been made to feel responsible by a parent or caregiver saying something like, "I've told you that you shouldn't wear your hair that way. Men find you attractive that way." Now the parent may have been trying to be "helpful", but how do you think most would hear that statement? Yep, as they are responsible for the situation happening. This is where shame begins.

Now let's say that Great Grandma has a baby girl...your Grandmother. Baby girl is born in the mid to late 1920s. What do you think she will receive from her mother emotionally? Well, probably not a lot. Great Grandma may have closed up emotionally because the situation taught her that she wasn't valued enough to be taken care of. If this was the case, she would have taken on shame and then likely passed it on to the baby girl. The behavior may appear to be a lack of emotion with her child, either verbally or physically. To be affirmed, a child needs love through words, as well as hugs and touch.

Your grandmother does not grow up with these affirmations and so therefore when she has a baby girl...your mother, what do you think she receives? Probably the same, right? If her mother did not receive a lot of love through words and touch she will not know how to give it to her. So, your mother did not receive that ability to give emotionally because she did not have a good example of it. So then, your mother has YOU. Guess what you get?

For example, if you were born in a time period after the 1960s, when society became more comfortable with talking about emotions, as well as public displays of affection, you saw a more forward approach and availability of "self-help" books. Now, for you, in the twenty-first century, you are sitting here looking for affirmation from your parents or caregivers and you feel empty. You ask yourself, "What's wrong with me?" "Why don't my parents love me?" "Why don't they like me?" You get the point.

The bottom line from this scenario is that you *may* be carrying shame that is four generations old and isn't even YOURS!! Your mother, your Grandmother and your Great Grandma DID NOT receive the (1) belief that emotions were important and (2) the example (behavior) to learn how to be emotional. Therefore, you may not have received it. It may have NOTHING to do with YOU. But, unfortunately that is exactly what we do. We take it personally!

Please also understand that back in the 1700-1800s, many families had children to have workers for the farm. The philosophy was very much about survival and getting the work done. There wasn't a whole lot of time or tolerance for a lot of emotion. That door really began to open in the 1960s.

The crucial point is that now you are an adult. Now it is YOUR responsibility and you can not be in a position of blame. You can understand where your situation is accountable to, but without blaming into the future. We can't change our past. It is a futile effort to stay in the past and hope for a different outcome. We now have to make a decision to learn from our past experience and use it to our best abilities.

Often, our old negative beliefs as well as the inability to face our own past will keep us in our system of blame. This is an immature action and an immature way of thinking. If we have the internal belief that we are not worthy, then it can cause us to have the feelings that we are not respected and externally we may act that out by not standing up for ourselves in a situation.

During childhood, we are given two types of messages; some verbal and others behavioral. For example, if a mother tells her daughter that she loves her but rarely hugs or embraces the young girl, this leaves the child doubting her worth. She may think to herself that she is not deserving of physical affection. The parent doesn't even have to tell the child that she is undeserving... the child receives the clear message through the behaviors.

This type of message can be given at any stage of developmental growth, even as an adult. For instance, the earlier story about my mother telling me I could be anything I wanted but not showing me how to go to school. Instead, intertwined were messages about her stripper friend who paid her way through school to become a lawyer.

So, let's start to break this down. As an individual, we have different aspects of who we are. We are made to be: mental, physical, emotional, spiritual and sexual. You can call these "states of being."

Mental State of Being

This is where you think. This represents your thoughts, beliefs and opinions. It is your mental state of being that processes information and makes decisions. Your mental state is important because you need to be healthy to process information correctly and be discerning about your situations.

Emotional State of Being

This state of being is where you have your emotions. This is where you feel or do not feel. Your emotional state of being helps with assessing feelings about others, often times having a "sense" of someone or a situation that may be harmful to us.

Spiritual State of Being

Your spiritual state of being is essentially your relationship to God. This is where you process your desire, your feelings and your knowledge of God.

Sexual State of Being

Your sexual state of being is where you have your belief system about yourself and others sexually. It has everything to do with the physical as well as emotional state and health of your sex life.

Physical State of Being

This is the state of being that has everything to do with the physical body. This is where boundaries are set with space and distance and touching.

Each one of these states of being is important to being complete, happy and at peace. You have all five of these on board. However, just because you have them does not mean that you are operating in them in a healthy manner. You may be healthy in one state of being but not in the other four or vice versa, you may be functioning well in four of them and only be off in one area. I know I have had clients that do the "oh well, at least the other areas of my life are okay." But if just one of these states of being is off balance and unhealthy in our lives, it can wreak havoc.

Think of this scenario. You may have been watching the news during a launching of the space shuttle when they were fearful that a tile on the shuttle may have fallen off. ONE TILE! Just one or several tiles on the spaceship are apparently so important that they can put in jeopardy a safe return. Can you imagine? I try to think of this enormously large ship that is approximately the size of a 13 story building and one "tile" can take the whole thing down. And, unfortunately, we have witnessed such tragedies.

The same is true in our own lives. We can be perfect at work, at church and with friends, but lead a very destructive romantic life. Well, that doesn't exactly charter our way to a peaceful life does it? However, I see many people get into this trap of thinking that just as long as 80% of their life is in control, they are good. But, they are left feeling empty or maybe even sad, angry, depressed or hopeless. This isn't good enough. We have to make the commitment to fulfilling peace in each area of our life.

The problem comes when we do not have self-control over one of these areas because we are allowing a negative internal belief which may cause us to relinquish our power. For instance, if you had a parent who told you they loved you but never hugged or showed you emotion, you may have received the message that you were not worthy of complete love. Therefore, in your emotional state of being, you may experience a low self-confidence and general low self-worth. Because of this internal feeling and belief, you may go out and try to find love from other places inappropriately. You may go through many relationships with none of them working and wonder why you cannot find love. You become even more lonely and sad which validates your internal belief about yourself. This is when confusion sets in.

Confusion is a dangerous feeling and needs to be recognized quickly. To me, confusion is when you allow someone to thrust their opinion, ideas or agenda on to you. Or, it is when you are weak in an area of one of your states of being and you take on the opinions, ideas or agenda of others because you are trying to fill a void. This is the behavior where we are trying to get acceptance and approval of others and are not thinking or feeling for ourselves. To start to identify if we are operating out of our own states of being or others, we have to first discover what old negative beliefs we are still allowing to run in our heads that propel us into this cycle.

So let's get started so that you can begin your change. Take a careful look through the list of negative beliefs. It is important to be honest with yourself. The beliefs below are things you either verbally heard or behaviorally were shown about who you "were." They could have come from caregivers, teachers or even a spouse. Understand that you may have received different messages than what I have provided, and so in a notebook, write those statements as well. This exercise may even take a few weeks as you look back on your experiences and history and start to open up your memory.

It is my personal belief that without working through your negative beliefs and turning them into positives, it will be difficult to make honest and clear changes in your life. As you look at these statements, I want you to hand write on the "My Current Negative Beliefs" page, the statements that you feel like you have on board. I believe it is important to hand write these and not just check mark them. When we hand write something, it makes it real and therefore it is our first step in admitting to ourselves our feelings and allows us to begin to start the real work ahead.

Old Belief List

I am not worthy

I am not pretty enough

I am not going to be successful

I don't deserve quality things in life

I am not skinny enough

I am not smart enough

I am unworthy of love

I am not talented

I do not make decisions well

I do not make decisions fast enough

I am ungrateful

I am negative

I don't deserve what I have

I will not find a suitable mate

I better marry this one; another one may not come along

If I need God, I'm weak

I am weak if I cry

I am weak if I show my feelings

I shouldn't stir things up

My place is to not say anything

I'm not athletic enough

I'm not feminine enough

I'm not masculine enough

I am a trouble-maker

If I hadn't come along, things would be different for my parents

I am too loud

I am too quiet

I don't show enough emotion

I show too much emotion

We don't hug/touch in this family

I am emotionally weak

I am too strong

I am a procrastinator

I am an inconvenience

I'm not a good listener

I am not a good communicator

I am manipulative

I cannot be alone

I am not good with people

My opinions don't matter

I am a failure

I don't fit in

There is not a place for me

I'm in the way

I don't have value

I am lazy

My Current Negative Beliefs

Hand write your current negative beliefs here:

1) _____

2) _____

3) _____

4) _____

5) _____

6) _____

7) _____

8) _____

9) _____

10) _____

As you can tell from the statements, these are not things that you want lurking in your mind. With thoughts like these, it is hard to be successful in different areas of your life whether it is in relationships, career or otherwise. So, we have to begin turning these around!! This is not easy and it does take time, as well as commitment.

I know that personally, I did not want to be wired and tired and feeling less than stellar about myself any longer. I committed my all to making myself a new person with new ideas and beliefs so that I could truly be happy and find peace. I knew the commitment was going to take some time, but I'd rather face myself and all the hard issues that come along with that, than to remain unhappy for a life time. The pay off was worth it to me to go through the immediate pain. Unfortunately though, I will from time to time come across a client who feels that it is just too painful to work on themselves and to face those things so they opt out and therefore opt out of ultimate happiness.

In order to find happiness and inner peace, we have to begin turning those old negative beliefs into positives. It will be next to impossible to truly find peace without doing so. Let's get started on doing that!

In a few pages you will find a section that says, "New Positive Beliefs." You are going to re-write every old negative belief into a positive one in this category. You will write these in "I am" statements. Do not use phrases like, "can, will, able, one day, going to," etc... Begin verbalizing these new beliefs as if they are already true. However old you are right now is how long your brain has heard those negative statements so understand that feeling these new positives won't happen overnight, but it will happen with commitment.

This is what the exercise may look like:

Old Belief	New Belief
I am not smart enough	I am smart and intelligent
I am not skinny enough	I am beautiful and whole
I am not worthy	I am worthy
I will not be successful	I am successful in all endeavors

You may also break the statements up by category:

BELIEF SYSTEM ABOUT WORTHINESS

OLD BELIEF:
I am unworthy of love

NEW BELIEF:
I am worthy and God fulfills my every need

OLD BELIEF:
I am a worthless person

NEW BELIEF:
I am a unique and special person

BELIEF SYSTEM ABOUT THE BODY

OLD BELIEF:
I am ugly

NEW BELIEF:
I am a beautiful person

OLD BELIEF:
I am fat

NEW BELIEF:
I am perfect just the way I am

BELIEF SYSTEM ABOUT RELATIONSHIPS

OLD BELIEF:
If I don't stay in this relationship another one may not come along

NEW BELIEF:
I attract healthy people into my life

OLD BELIEF:
My mate will eventually leave me

NEW BELIEF:
I loving and lasting relationships

BELIEF SYSTEM ABOUT INTELLIGENCE

OLD BELIEF:
I am stupid and dumb

NEW BELIEF:
I am intelligent and resourceful

OLD BELIEF:
I am a slow individual

NEW BELIEF:
I am a smart and unique person

You might also make a guideline for what you will offer to your developing relationships. These can be things that you would like to contribute that would nurture yourself and the relationship. A guideline helps us to stay in check with our behavior. We need to look at things such as co-dependent or care-giving behavior. Let's take a look at some of the things we can affirm to ourselves.

EXAMPLES:

1) I share my feelings with my partner
2) I am honest and straight forward with my partner
3) I am nurturing to my partner
4) I listen to my partner's needs and wants
5) I take care of my financial responsibilities
6) I desire to increase my knowledge and education
7) I relax and have fun showing my self-confidence
8) I have faith in God and share those feelings with my partner
9) I am continually working on my self-development
10) I use my boundaries appropriately when needed

Once you have completed all of your new positive belief statements, I want you to read them every day either upon waking up or before bed. This begins re-framing your mindset. At first, it is going to be like lipstick on a pig. The pig is still ugly. What I mean by this is that at first, you won't necessarily believe the new positive statements about yourself and as you are reading them you may even think it's a lie. But, repetition is the key to believing.

Along with repetition of reading these daily, you will need to be on a self-development path in which you are working on yourself whether it is through working with a coach, mentor, pastor, therapist, reading books, going to classes or some other means. You need to be doing something regularly each week. So with these two working in conjunction, it is amazing over time how someone will begin to take on these new positive beliefs. It may take as long as a year or more for you to be able to begin believing these new positives about yourself, but don't give up. Remember, you have had the old beliefs on board for many years.

Rewrite your NEW positive beliefs here:

My NEW Positive Beliefs

1) _____

2) _____

3) _____

4) _____

5) _____

6) _____

7) _____

8) _____

9) _____

10) _____

I have had many clients come to me who say they have a negative belief in God and that they would like to change that. That is a heavy task. It is one that I understand. When I first started working with my coach, I did not have a belief in a higher power. I couldn't even say "Jesus." If I did, "freak" had to come right after it. That is how detached I was from any kind of spirituality. My parents were night club entertainers back in the 1940s, 50s and 60s. They had quite a chaotic and dysfunctional lifestyle.

My mother had been raised by her mother, who had a lot of religious abuse on board that she extended over to my mother. It didn't help that my mother also had her pastor at age fourteen try to make a sexual pass towards her. You can imagine how this tainted her belief about spirituality, as well as church itself. It would assure that my siblings and I would not be raised with any type of spiritual groundwork.

My coach having this information knew that I would not take on positive change as fast. It's not that I couldn't, but humans tend to learn and adapt faster when they have a belief in a higher power. So, he decided that it was time for me to "get a God." Being a Christian himself, he was led by God to have me to do an assignment that some may not initially approve of or may think is sacrilegious. Please consider I had NO religion or God on board in the first place. So, his risk was minimal and he was obeying what God told him.

My coach had me "make up a God that I was comfortable with accepting." Yep, you heard that right. I got to make up EXACTLY what I wanted in a God. At first, this was a very hard and painful exercise. Just like with the "new beliefs", I didn't believe in this new God right away. But, I created my list and I read the statements every day. Here is an example of some of the ones that were in my journal when I "created" my God.

- She loves me no matter what I do, right or wrong
- She accepts me no matter what I feel or think
- She is with me every second of the day so if I need her she will be there for me
- She is honest with me and never lies or covers up anything
- When I cannot handle a problem or situation she helps me and takes care of it for me
- She is always loving to me and understanding

- She affirms to me that it is not my job to care take and that it is acceptable to not be perfect
- She will never leave me

Okay, you may be thinking… "she?" This was safe for me when I first wrote these out in 1991. The great news is that a couple years later while working through my issues and reading these new beliefs about God, I began to replacing "She" with "He," realizing that this was truly God. This began a process for me where it became safe to believe in God. However, it took time, like the rest of my self-beliefs. No matter how old you are right now, you have had that many years of negative thinking about yourself. Individuals get very anxious and feel like they should be able to solve it upon discovery. It is simply not that easy. We have to begin to uncover how we got there and then change these messages.

Behaviors That Can Be Taken On By Negative Beliefs:

One of the behaviors negative beliefs can instill in us is perfectionism. For those that were made to feel or heard that they didn't measure up, this is often their route to trying to fix this dilemma. However, most perfectionists just find themselves on the hamster wheel of approval, feeling as if they cannot get off.

There are generally two types of perfectionism: internal and external. Internal perfectionism comes from our not having a healthy self-worth and it tells us that we need to do something to live up to expectations. With internal perfectionism, we often feel anxiety, unlovable, in the way, don't fit in, don't measure up, never going to be good enough and the messages go on.

With external perfectionism, we usually feel fine about ourselves, but it's others we are not always keen with. In this level of perfectionism, we are often frustrated with others who do not measure up to our standard. These individuals may have come from parents who over stated their worth and built a false expectation for others outside of themselves. You can have traits of both internal and external perfectionism. It is important to evaluate both and make sure you understand what traits may fall within you. We become a perfectionist in a couple different ways. One, we can receive messages from things that were said to us such as:

- You never do it right!
- What were you thinking doing it that way
- You were just not meant to be book smart
- You never...
- You are an average student
- Shouldn't you have...
- "Sally just has her special way of doing things" (hint the sarcasm)

Secondly, behaviors also play a big role in teaching us that we don't live up, causing someone to potentially act out their perfectionism for acceptance. You may exhibit it in behaviors like:

- Repeatedly watching someone re-do something you just did
- Always having to wear the right outfit
- Not being able to go out without makeup on
- Working out excessively
- Not being able to rest until all work or chores are done

It is an important step in your process to exactly identify how you may be acting out your perfectionism. Use the space below to write out how you learned messages both verbally and behaviorally.

Verbal messages said to me: **Who said it:**

_____   _____

_____   _____

_____   _____

Behavioral messages shown to me: **Who showed them to me:**

_____   _____

_____   _____

_____   _____

Now identify what you feel are the verbal messages you currently tell yourself about being perfect:

_____

_____

_____

_____

_____

_____

Now identify what you feel are the behaviors that you're exhibiting that keeps you in your perfectionism.

_____

_____

_____

_____

_____

_____

One of the reasons we have issues with changing our behaviors is that we have a hard time admitting the internal belief and where it came from. Many individuals have guilt that they are somehow dishonoring their parents or caregivers by admitting that they may have been wrong. This prevents many people from seeking a higher level of self and therefore struggling to get to that goal of inner peace.

I realize the acknowledgement is difficult. We want to think that our parents were perfect and if we admit anything otherwise, it makes us wrong. It doesn't necessarily make us wrong; sometimes it just makes us uneducated. You have to understand this for your parents as well. Your parents didn't necessarily decide they were going to say or do things to make you feel like you had to be perfect. They themselves may have felt the same way because it was passed down through generations and no one really knows where it started. Just like the "Great Grandma example," we often "carry" behaviors and beliefs of others when they aren't even ours to carry. This is how shame enters our lives.

To me I call shame the sludge of the earth. It is a bottom feeder. There is no lower point. Shame to me is the feeling that *"something is wrong with me!"* That can be devastating. We have to understand the difference between guilt and shame. Guilt is a feeling of being responsible for something you should or should not have done. Usually, but not always, you can work past guilt fairly quickly and begin to move forward. Many times people confuse guilt with shame. Shame is a feeling that is often harbored for a long period of time and is very difficult to shake. If you feel "something is wrong with me", it is hard to have good beliefs about yourself which can trigger the perfection behavior. You can see now how you get on the hamster wheel.

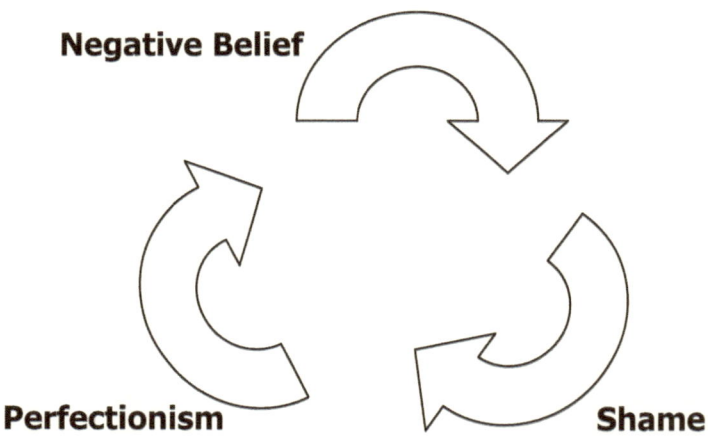

Negative Belief

Perfectionism

Shame

You may never be able to identify "why you are this way." Though I find many people have some clues about how they got there. However, sometimes there is information that we just do not have access to and instead of accepting that there must have been a source, we blame ourselves. "I'm just hard on myself." Granted, there are some people with a natural personality that tends to be more driven and will come off as if they are being harder on themselves. The difference is, they usually enjoy being like this. It is what motivates them. What we have to ask is, "Are we happy?" That is the barometer for whether or not your "perfectionism" has gone too far or is within the normal confines of your overdriven personality.

It is one of the hardest things for people to do, to set aside the "have to know" factor. We all want to know why or how we got here, but sometimes, in order to fix the issue, we have to just accept that WE ARE HERE and begin dealing with the behaviors. You may not remember exactly what your parents said to you or how they showed things to you through their behaviors. The important thing is to not beat yourself up about it and to begin working through the process of change.

This is a journey for you to take on for YOURSELF and no one else. Often times when we are healing we want others to heal with us. We get an epiphany and feel like we have to share it with everyone around us. The bottom line is that others will have a hard time if you start getting in their business. You must fix yourself first and then just be an example to others. You cannot fix anyone outside of yourself. The journey has to start with you!

Did you ever notice when you were a teen growing up you swore you would never be like your parents? That you would do better? Yet, you discovered once you became an adult and a parent that you some-how sound and act just like your parents. You realize that not much has changed in your life except your home and surroundings and possibly the people around you. However, we are playing out the same role we had as children and are now taking on the behaviors and patterns of our parents or peers who brought us up. How does this happen? What happened to that motivation of change and individuality? Or, are we in a state of denial?

Since I was from a family of dysfunction, I was brought up in much shame. Shame, I believe, is where family secrets begin. I did not want to let others know what these circumstances were. What would people think? Shame bound me from my quest for truth until I woke up to my misery. Family secrets don't have to hold us back. We have to decide how much is too much and take a stand to do something about it.

The one most important thing that we're either not told or that we often forget is that we have a CHOICE. Yes, a choice. Imagine that! Sounds impossible at times and believe it or not, it is true. We choose in life what is going to happen. You ask, "How can that be?" I believe we choose situations in life that we need to learn from. Have you ever noticed that you attract the same situations over and over until one day you decide, "I don't have to do it like this anymore." You are tired of suffering and paying the price, so, you make a change, almost as if one day you wake up and make a conscious decision that things will be different this time.

I believe so many people are afraid of making a choice and acting on it is because they fear failure. As children growing up, we must learn responsibility and morality. To learn these things we have to begin to make choices on our own. If we were shown by our parents that it is okay to make mistakes and that is the way we sometimes have to learn, it makes sense that we would have an easier time as an adult making choices. However, if parents continually ridicule and shame children for making the wrong choices, it is understandable that when these children grow up, they may have a large amount of fear in making choices and fear of feeling like a failure.

THERE ARE POSITIVES IN EVERY CHOICE! Imagine that concept. And it's true. Let's suppose you make a decision and it doesn't work out the way you planned it. Well, take a look at the situation. There is a lesson to be learned out of every choice you make. It all depends on how you CHOOSE to let the situation affect you.

Take the worst possible situation that could happen. Now, ask yourself how you would let it affect you. Would you let it devastate you or would you try and learn from the situation and pull yourself up, dust yourself off and try again? It is all up to you because it is YOUR CHOICE. No one can take that away from you, unless you give the choice away.

So, if we have a choice for things to be the way we want them, why do we continue to stay in unsatisfying situations? Why do we give up our choices? It is true that we are creatures of habit; however, we need to take responsibility for why we are creatures of habit. If we were not creatures living out of habit, then that would only mean one thing: We are creatures of change. Haven't heard of many of those, have you?

We give up our choice because we DO NOT BELIEVE we have one. Again, it goes back to our belief system. Take an oath today that you are going to begin a new belief system for yourself. You can choose to continue to be unhappy, unfulfilled, wired and tired or you can choose to do something about it.

Oath Of Peace & Happiness

I, _____, am choosing today to work on myself to become a happy, fulfilled, energetic and peaceful person. I acknowledge that I am WORTH IT!

I will not give up the fight to obtain my goals and dreams.

I am deserving of loving relationships, kindness towards me and peace.

I am worthy of greatness in my life.

I have a place in this world and will create that atmosphere for myself.

I will measure up to my goals and dreams and let go of unhealthy expectations.

I will play and smile more.

I will act boldly in my actions towards change.

I will seek the answers to better my life.

I will love myself!

Signed_____Date_____

Looking At CHANGE In Order To Obtain NEW BELIEFS

In the dictionary, the definition of change almost goes on for half a page. It is amazing that we try to avoid change so much when it has so much substance and depth to the meaning. Change looks like so many different things and can be applied to so many aspects of our lives. We cannot grow without changing. Children, if you watch them, get so excited when they are presented with something new.

Change also means new, maybe something we haven't experienced before. Maybe we perceive change negatively. I've noticed that as we grow out of childhood, the excitement seems to switch into fear. Throughout my life I've seen a lot of people take change very hard. As if nothing will ever be right again. It just won't be the same. It doesn't necessarily mean it has to be wrong. I believe there is no right and wrong, just change. We can take it however we want to. Imagine, again we have a choice!

Change sometimes means giving up something that has been a part of us our entire lifetime. That can be very difficult. However, to live a functional and healthy life, sometimes it means that we must make that difficult change in our life to make it better for ourselves and/or our children or marriage. You have to look at what good will come out of the change you are considering and look ahead. During difficult times, such as a change or having to make a difficult choice, it may help if you seek support from a group, friend, or counselor. Communicating our problems, needs, and wants is crucial to our happiness and serenity. Taking a positive outlook on a situation can help turn things around. What will you get out of obtaining a new POSITIVE belief system?

Saying and expressing what we feel means having good communication skills. As babies, we are perfect. If we want or need something, we communicate it. Babies aren't afraid to communicate the need for food, love, or attention. If they are unhappy, believe me, you will be the first to know about it. If you notice, almost immediately, an adult is there telling us that expressing our feelings, needs, and wants is inappropriate. We are "hushed" or told to stop crying, or we will get in trouble. No wonder we have difficulty as adults expressing our feelings when the only time we are able to express them is when it is convenient for someone else.

We learn there are conditions in which we can express ourselves. Did you watch your father tell your mother, "Not now Honey, I'm watching the football game?" Maybe your father goes to give the mother a kiss and she says, "Not in front of the children."

These kinds of messages told me that I had to be careful when choosing to express my feelings. It is also important that we have proper sexual communication in the household besides just conversational and emotional communication. Remember we have five "states of being." The states of being again are: mental, emotional, physical, spiritual and sexual. All areas need open and honest communication. There are many forms of communication. I never saw my parents being affectionate, so I took on the belief that it is inappropriate to be affectionate. This, of course, can develop into serious relationship problems when trying to be intimate with a partner. As you see, methods of communication develop our beliefs.

These communication skills or lack of communication skills, are passed from generation to generation if not changed. That is why, if we become aware of ineffective behavior, we need to make a change if planning on influencing our children differently. Even if you choose not to have children, do you want to continue living in ineffective patterns?

Communicating With a New Belief System

If our experiences have not been good when communicating with others, we may feel like we've been bitten and become reluctant to express ourselves to others.

I was about to graduate from high school and even though my father had not been around most of my life, I still wanted him to come to my graduation ceremony. When I expressed my feelings to my mother, she had a different idea.

She criticized me for wanting what she said was a "no good, two timing, child support skipping, good for nothing father" to come to my graduation. She also told me that if I invited him to my high school graduation she would not be there. As you can imagine, I felt devastated. Not only did I feel a tremendous amount of anger towards my mother, I also felt like I should crawl under a rock and hide for wanting my father at my graduation. I felt shameful and guilty.

Because of the care-taking situation I was brought up in, I wasn't encouraged to communicate appropriately. I felt like I couldn't jeopardize the roof over my head, even though I had been working since I was thirteen. I uninvited my father to my graduation, and we did not speak for nearly four years.

At an early age, I learned that it was not okay to express my feelings in any manner...this is a belief taken on. Instead, I was shown how to manipulate and control to get what I needed or wanted. I learned how to be an actress instead of an honest kid showing my feelings. Growing up around my family meant getting better at hiding my feelings, manipulating, and controlling others. Even though it was never a conscious decision to interact with others in this way, it was a means of survival. It was the communication form I learned.

My mother was proud of me and encouraged me when it benefited her. One evening, my father had called drunk, and once again, he got into one of his beloved accusatory conversations about my mother. I let it rip. I told him that if the things he accused my mother of were true, then I didn't blame her because he was such a terrible person. I yelled at him about his abandonment, his drinking, his womanizing and anything else that came to mind. Of course, he couldn't hear me over all of the excuses. My mother sat there and was beaming with pride watching her thirteen year old daughter defend her mother's honor. Communication was one-sided, manipulative, and rarely honest. Obviously I was given the belief that this behavior was not only acceptable, but that it would be rewarded.

Communication is the glue that holds relationships together. Communication has to come from all parties involved. In business transactions, all parties have to communicate wants and needs to be able to reach a contractual agreement. Why would anyone think that they can get away without communicating in a relationship? Communication isn't an area where everyone is skilled. It takes discipline, courage, desire, motivation, and practice, as well as a new set of beliefs so that the communication is appropriate.

I assert that at times, all of us have probably been, or are in a relationship, where no matter how much we try to get our mate to communicate, it just doesn't work. This can be very frustrating and is probably the leading cause of divorce. It is my experience that having a relationship is almost impossible to maintain without good communication. Listening is just as important as communicating. It is often hard to listen though, because we may not like the things we hear. We usually don't like what we hear when there is some truth involved.

You may have a perfectly fine belief system about communicating, but if your spouse doesn't, it makes it difficult to successfully communicate. You see the problem.

When someone is communicating with you, be patient and be present--meaning: listen to what they are telling you. It may be very difficult for the person to open up and expose their feelings to you. Communicating can often feel very vulnerable. Respect the person for their willingness and effort. A lot of looking away, fidgeting, and interrupting may send a message to a person that they are not being heard. If the person is exhibiting that behavior towards you, it may be a signal that they are uncomfortable or that they are being disrespectful.

No matter how difficult it is to hear something, always try to look at the person as they are talking. This really lets a person know they are being heard. Let the person completely finish what they have to say. It is very tempting to interrupt when we hear something we don't like. Let the other person share their feelings with you until it is your turn to share yours. However, do not use your talk time to get even with the person for what they have said. You want to be treated as an adult and adults need to listen.

Your communication time is not to convince the person that everything they have just said is not true. It is true for them because it is their feelings. This can be very difficult to remember in moments of intense conversation. One helpful way to prevent yourself from disparaging another person's feelings is by repeating back to the person what they have just said--a brief synopsis of what they have said, highlighting the key points, is sufficient.

If the person agrees that you have heard correctly, then you have an opportunity to communicate. If the individual feels that they have been heard incorrectly, then they get an opportunity to repeat those things they feel you did not hear. There must be a lot of patience in this process and it may take several times for the person to feel you received the data correctly.

When you communicate, try using short sentences with understandable words. You are not trying to win a contest in proper English. Speak slowly or moderately to be fully heard. Express your feelings and thoughts as you feel comfortable. Tell the person what they did to you and how you feel about it. Give your facts, and do not blame. You are trying to get across how you feel about something they may have done.

Don't expect to change the person's mind about anything. This is not the point; the point is to communicate your feelings, set boundaries if necessary and establish grounds for resolving an issue and establishing your wants and needs in the relationship. You are a loving, deserving person. You are entitled to the very best, including having great communication in a loving relationship. If these simple steps do not work, you may have a deeper level communication issue and may want to seek a third party for help.

Let's look at a mock conversation below to observe healthy communication.

SPEAKER:

When you left me and moved out without communicating with me, I felt hurt by your actions. I felt betrayed by you, which created my anger towards you. I also felt terrified of being alone and desperate for what to do. I felt embarrassed and too ashamed to tell anyone. I don't understand why you felt you couldn't communicate to me what you were feeling and the problems you were having with the relationship. I'd like for you to tell me.

PARTNER:

I heard you say you were hurt and felt betrayed and so you are angry with me. You were scared of being alone and you didn't want to tell anyone.

The speaker did not feel as if she was heard completely by her partner so she will repeat the items he did not hear.

SPEAKER:

I also told you that I felt embarrassed and ashamed and I was terrified, not just scared. I experienced these feelings as a result of you leaving me without communicating your feelings to me. I want you to communicate with me now the problems that led you to leave.

PARTNER:

You felt embarrassed and ashamed. You were terrified. You felt these things because I left you and didn't talk to you about it. You now want me to tell you how I feel and why I left.

The speaker feels she was heard and is now satisfied with what she has communicated. Now, the partner has the opportunity to express his feelings and the speaker will listen and repeat back to the partner what she heard. You may not be able to resolve the problem; however, both parties will feel much better that their feeling are out on the table.

Communication is a very complex issue within itself and an entire book can be devoted to this topic alone. Please remember though that poor communication starts because (1) the person was not SHOWN behaviorally how to communicate and (2) may have beliefs on board about communication that are not positive. When we have positive beliefs we are going to communicate in a more effective manner.

One of the ways to ensure better communication is to identify where you need improvement. List out on the next page, in each state of being, how you feel like you need to improve your level of communication.

Mental State of Being

_____

_____

Emotional State of Being

_____

_____

Spiritual State of Being

_____

_____

Sexual State of Being

_____

_____

_____

Physical State of Being

_____

_____

You can see through this chapter that there is a lot to consider in the realm of "beliefs" and how many areas of our lives it can affect. Beliefs are deep seeded and we need to get a clear understanding of how we learned them in order to effectively make change. We have to understand what was said to us, that we took on as a belief. We have to understand the actions towards us from others that behaviorally showed us who we are and formed our belief system. In all of these things; words, behaviors, lack of understanding we have a choice, fear of change, and our communication methods have put us on a collision course that has left us in a mangled mess called: CHAOS. It leaves us wired and tired and desiring peace we have not understood how to achieve.

Now that we have uncovered so much under the beliefs chapter, I am excited for you that your life can begin changing through this process if you choose to do the work. Let's recap your action steps from Chapter 1-Beliefs, so that you have a full understanding of what you will need to accomplish.

____ Determine and write your OLD negative beliefs

____ Write your NEW positive beliefs

____ Write out verbal negative beliefs you received

____ Write out behavioral negative beliefs you received

____ Write the negative messages you are telling yourself

____ Write the negative behaviors you are currently exhibiting

____ Take the Oath of Peace & Happiness

____ Identify areas of communication you need to improve

Chapter 2

Boundaries

Whatever we do, we should do as unto the Lord, not unto ourselves. The Lord is not a heavy task master. His yoke is easy and His burden is light. (matt. 11:30)

Lack of boundaries: this is where one becomes wired and tired, feeling anxious and left feeling empty and without peace. Boundaries are an essential part of the 3 B's equation. Without good beliefs, you will not set boundaries in your life. And without boundaries in your life, you cannot have balance. It is as simple as that. So we first have to make sure we have the right beliefs on board to begin working on our boundaries.

Essentially, boundaries are behaviors. In order to have balance we have to have the proper boundaries in place. We have to be able to say "no", we have to pay our bills, stand up for ourselves, not touch people inappropriately or allow inappropriate touching, give opinions when appropriate, not be mean, etc. ... as you can imagine, the list can go on.

Boundaries are one of the harder things to establish in self-development. It is hard to say "no" or set limitations with people when you have always given yourself to others. I really knew I was making changes in my life and doing great when I was able to successfully set boundaries with others and more importantly, keep them. Setting boundaries isn't just about saying "no." It is about establishing yourself with others.

Boundaries are set around your wants, needs, values, and beliefs and being comfortable. Boundaries are where you end and I begin.

When you say "yes" to something that you really wanted to say "no" to, how do you feel? I noticed when I first started self-development I was used to letting others have their way. I didn't like it; however, I didn't resist it. Over time, the more I studied and worked on this issue, the more it became not okay to say "yes" all the time. I realized I deserved to have things my way. The more I made my own decisions, the more I felt like my own person. To set boundaries, you have to own your own state of being. When our self-esteem is low and we don't own our state of being, then it will be difficult to set and keep boundaries.

Much of the time humans want to control their situation or the situation of others in order to have peace in their lives. Unbeknownst to them until they encounter it, it just tends to wreak havoc in their lives instead. Often individuals don't even know they are being controlling or inappropriate with their boundaries.

There are those that are caught up in the behavior because it is learned and then there are those that are out right manipulative, and well, that is a whole other book within itself. Basically though, we are talking about the person who may be a narcissist, or even sociopathic in nature. These individuals are not only calculating and ego driven but with sociopaths they do not have a conscience and so therefore will take risks that the normal individual would not dream of doing. Most times, neither of these types of personality disorders have a clear understanding of appropriate boundaries. However, neither does the person with the learned negative behaviors until the appropriate boundaries are learned.

There are two types of boundaries. The first is internal. This has everything to do with the chatter that goes on in your head. This is where your internal beliefs hang out. Now you see why you have to identify and begin tackling the internal beliefs first. Without recognizing them, it is hard to set appropriate boundaries. Internal boundaries are also your thoughts, ideas and opinions.

The internal boundaries make up feeling, thinking, and action. This boundary is about being accountable. How you feel, think, and act is up to you, and no one can make you be any different unless you give into them. How you feel, think, and act is about YOU and what another person feels, thinks, and acts is about THEM. This boundary is very important to understand. When a person is co-dependent, they do not understand this boundary. A co-dependent person will become enmeshed with other individuals' feelings, thoughts, and actions. When you do not have internal boundaries, it becomes difficult, often impossible, to express your needs and wants.

Being co-dependent and without internal boundaries, I tended to keep blaming others for the things that went wrong in my life. People do not like to be continually blamed for things. Relationships can't survive under such pressure. Be accountable for who you are and what you need and want.

Strong boundaries attract strong people who will admire your self-love and self-esteem. When we are not using boundaries, we will attract people who don't have boundaries. Like many other things, setting internal boundaries is a skill that takes time to develop and execute. When you set a boundary with someone, the person you have set it with does not have the option to discuss it or reach a compromise. If you feel comfortable with setting a boundary with someone, do not allow them to pressure you to change your mind. This is your boundary with them. They do not get to control it.

External boundaries have everything to do with your physical body and space. It deals with touch, feeling and the need for appropriate personal space with others. Many may think it would be crazy if you didn't set physical boundaries; however, many individuals do not feel they have a right to their own body. They may say one thing and act out another. This comes from low self-esteem and skewed data. It is important to know that you do have every right over your body, and do not let anyone tell you differently. If you find an individual telling you differently, then they are more than likely trying to manipulate you. This is a good time to set a boundary. Stand up for yourself and your body.

I remember when I first started setting physical boundaries. It wasn't always the easiest thing to do. One night I was at a party with a couple of girlfriends and a man walked in who was very attractive. He glanced my way and came over. As he began to talk I could tell he had had too much to drink. He almost immediately put a hand on my butt.

I instantly grabbed his hand firmly, took it off of my body and said, "You do not have my permission to touch me; however, you can stand here and talk to me." It was quite a sight. His jaw dropped and he just backed up and left with his buddies; I'm sure to discuss what a witch I was. I'll never forget how proud I was of myself and how good I felt to tell someone not to violate my body. When you set healthy boundaries, celebrate yourself for doing so, as well as celebrating others when they have to set boundaries with you.

Some individuals may feel that because they are married, they do not have a right to set boundaries with their spouses concerning their body. Just because you are married doesn't mean you don't have the right to set boundaries. Your body is still yours and you have a choice as to who touches you and where, when, and how.

I feel that it is a matter of respect to honor someone else's decisions and boundaries, including a spouse. When setting boundaries with a spouse, let them know that you have your best interest in mind. You do love them and you appreciate their understanding. When someone has set a boundary with you, it is understandable that you may become somewhat insecure until you develop skills of setting boundaries and owning your reality. Communication is the key.

Both of these boundaries are important to understand and they often work together. For instance, if you have the internal belief that you are unlovable, you may become a promiscuous person. You may want to say no in the moment but something inside tells you, "He won't like me any more if I don't allow him to touch me." So, you see where this lack of internal boundary affects the external boundary. They then get tied together.

Basic external boundaries without internal messages enforced may be:

- someone patting you on the butt without permission
- standing too close to you
- hugging you without asking
- grabbing your arm to show you something
- playing "footsie" with you under the table…when you aren't playing

You get the point; what it looks like when someone does not have an understanding of another individual's external boundaries. However, if you do not say something to this individual and correct them on their behavior, then most likely you have an internal boundary that is not functioning. If you have a healthy internal boundary you will speak up for yourself and set an appropriate external boundary with the individual.

A lack of internal boundaries is a direct result of the beliefs you have on board. Remember, our beliefs turn into behaviors. We tend to act out how we feel or think on the inside. Let me take you through an activity that will help explain this. This will be an activity for you to complete.

You will see the graphic of a tree provided in the next few pages. I like to think of this tree as a person. Within that person we have roots. At the root of who we are is what we think about ourselves, our beliefs. Every belief we have about our self is going to make us feel a certain way whether we are aware of it are not. This is where a lot of the problem begins. First, we don't know the negative beliefs that we still have on board about ourselves and therefore don't admit the feeling we have because of that belief.

Trust me; if you have bad beliefs about yourself, you are going to have a bad feeling. If you have good beliefs about yourself, you will have a good feeling. So, I like to call this an unexposed feeling. Think about how often you see an "angry type" of person walk around admitting they are an "angry type" of person. Most will loudly deny that they are angry. Yet, you see it. You walk into a room and see "that" person who is angry or "that" person who seems like a "wounded bird" as if they have a lot of sadness.

The internal negative belief and the unexposed feeling are the roots below the surface in this graphic. They are the things we don't often expose to others even though people may figure it out. We are usually the ones that are not willing to admit it.

Above "ground" in our graphic is where you start to see the base and trunk of the tree. This is what we expose to others. This is where we exhibit our behaviors. Everyone can see those behaviors even though sometimes we may not. But, I consider these to be more visible not only to others, but to our eye as well, if we are in admittance. I often hear people say, "I don't know why I do this, I just do." They know what the behavior is; they just don't know why they are doing it. They have yet to discover the drive of the behavior…the internal negative belief as well as the unexposed feeling.

In our graphic you notice a nice bushy tree with fruit and above the tree in the heavens we have our goal. The problem is that if we keep any negative beliefs on board, along with the unexposed feeling and negative behaviors, what happens to the fruit that gets us to our goal? You got it. It withers, dies and falls to the ground. Our goal is out of reach.

Think about it this way, a person has a constant weight challenge. They go through diet after diet, but gain the weight back each time. At no time did they do any internal work on their beliefs or their unexposed feeling and so therefore, the behavior can't change permanently. It may change temporarily, but it eventually reverts back to its original behavior. So, the goal of keeping the weight off is never achieved. This brings unhappiness to our lives and can often reinforce our negative internal beliefs. Hence, the hamster wheel.

Going through the negative internal belief exercise you may have uncovered multiple negative beliefs. You would need to process through this tree graphic for EACH negative belief. Remember, like the space shuttle, if one thing is missing or off, we cannot expect a positive result.

Let's take a look at a few examples of how to work through this tree of peace. Because I know that you may be "numb" and don't know how you feel or what behaviors you are exhibiting, I included a feeling/behavior list for you to reference after the "tree" graphics. While you are working through the trees, flip back and forth to reference this tool. It is important that you clearly define not only your unexposed feeling but all of the behaviors you want to change. You will draw this out on paper. My husband drew the following 4 illustrations as an example of how you would progress within the tree. Of course, you will only fill out one "tree" per negative internal belief. You do not have to be as detailed on your illustration of the tree…it is just a tool for understanding.

Graphic 1: Identify Goal You Seek

Goal ___INNER PEACE___

Behaviors _____

Unexposed feeling _____
Internal belief _____

Graphic 2: Identify Internal Negative Belief

Goal INNER PEACE

Behaviors

Unexposed feeling

Internal belief I AM UNLOVABLE

Graphic 3: Identify Your Unexposed Feeling

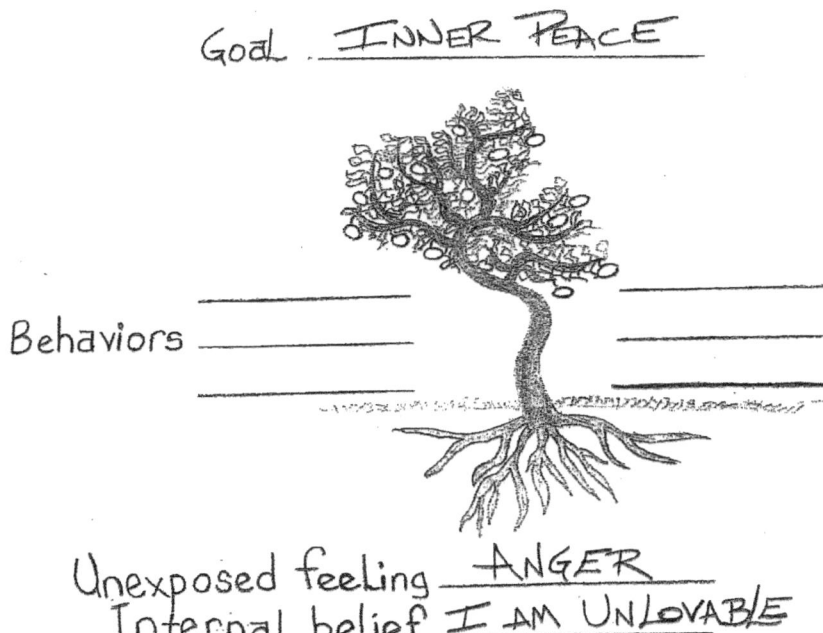

Goal INNER PEACE

Behaviors

Unexposed feeling ANGER
Internal belief I AM UNLOVABLE

Graphic 4: Identify Your Unhealthy Behaviors That Keep You From Your Goal

Goal ___INNER PEACE___

Behaviors

LOUD
SARCASTIC
DISTANT

SNAPPY
RUDE
UN-TRUSTING

Unexposed feeling ___ANGER___
Internal belief ___I AM UNLOVABLE___

Feeling/Behavior Words

abandoned	emotionless	nervous
absorbed	edgy	numb
affectionate	exhausted	open
angry	fearful	overwhelmed
agony/dread	frustrated	optimistic
apprehensive	fragile	passionate
alienated	fulfilled	peaceful
appreciative	friendly	people pleaser
anxious	grateful	proud
beat down	grief	panicked
boundary-less	guilty	pretending
burnt out	hate	regret/remorse
burdened	hurt	resentful
calm	happy	restless
clear headed	hopeless	relaxed
comfortable	helpless	sympathetic
centered	hostile	sad
confused	indifferent	satisfied
compassionate	impatient	safe
denial	irritable	shame
distant	indecisive	stressed out
distracted	insecure	suspicious
disgruntled	interested	self-conscious
disturbed	involved	sensitive
depressed	jealous	shaky
despair	liar	troubled
disappointed	lethargic	trusting
discouraged	lonely	thankful
disgusted	lost	uncomfortable
egotistical	loving	uninterested
empowered	longing	unhappy
expectant	loud/quiet	unworthy
encouraged	low self-confidence	upset
enablerenergetic	mistrustful	withdrawn
enthusiastic	miserable	worried
embarrassed	needy	

One of the things that we have to identify when learning how to set boundaries is to recognize our non-accepting behaviors. These behaviors will keep us in our dysfunction and away from our goals. One of those goals may be to obtain peace. For example:

- If you are overweight and continue to buy junk food
- If you are a shopaholic and continue going to the mall
- You are in debt but refuse to open the bills
- You keep showing up at your boyfriend's house even though he doesn't pay attention to you and continues to treat you poorly
- You continue doing errands for a friend though she does not show you any gratitude

In each of these scenarios, you can see that there is a mental block that is going on and that the person is refusing to look at the situation and what is really taking place. This behavior can occur because the person is afraid to expose the internal negative belief they have about themselves. However, until discovered, it will remain and the goal of peace eludes us.

This is bold work. The journey is not easy. We have to admit things about ourselves and others that are not pleasant, but are necessary to achieve the goal. As part of this admission, we have to ask ourselves a question that we might think we have the answer to but have to do a bit of soul searching to admit the truth. That question is, "Am I currently taking action to improve this area or am I not?" Often times we are aware of our issues but are not doing anything about it.

One of the reasons this step is so important is that we have to acknowledge our participation in the issue. Whether that participation is in-action or even actions that are non-accepting behaviors as previously listed. Our life issues are often driven by the internal beliefs we are carrying, as well as our reaction to those issues. If you had the internal belief of, "I'm not worthy of quality time with others," then you may ignore your own needs and your behaviors may exhibit that belief in not paying your bills, not making friendships, etc.

Complete the following activity: " Boundaries Inventory Graph," (on the following pages) to assist you in determining how your current life issues may be linked to your past, as well as help you understand how you are or are not participating in your own personal healing.

Look at the example chart as a guide and review the instructions below on how to fill it out.

How to fill it out:

State of being
Under each state of being in the blank space write out the issue. For instance:

State of being:
Physical
Issue: Gained 20 pounds

External/Internal:
Write an "E" or an "I" whether it is an external or internal issue. For instance, if it were someone inappropriately touching you and you were afraid to tell them to stop because you were afraid of what they would think about you, this would be an internal boundary issue. So, then you would write an "I". Understand that some issues may be both external as well as internal. For instance, if you gained 20 pounds since they put a snack machine right outside of your office, that is a new external issue, but it is lack of an internal boundary that allows you to continually go to the snack machine.

Action/Inaction:
Write an "A" or an "I" whether you are taking action or inaction about the situation. This is a crucial step to admitting your participation level in the situation, and is one of the healthiest and healing things you can do. It gets us out of denial and allows us to step into the action phase faster.

Non-Accepting Behaviors:
In this space list any non-accepting behaviors you may be performing to avoid the situation. For instance, if you are in debt and you are not opening your bills because of fear. Not opening them is a non-accepting behavior.

Belief:

We must tie in our beliefs to our behaviors because of course this is where our problem lies and perpetuates the situation. Look back at your negative behavior list you wrote out and correlate what you feel is the belief that keeps you in this behavior.

Action:

Within this space, begin to write out solutions that you feel you could begin taking action on. Whether it is working with a coach, mentor, therapist, reading books or taking classes, action is the key to working through these issues. If you have a hard time looking for answers, work with someone to assist you with solutions. But be sure you are WILLING TO TAKE ACTION on the solutions they are assisting you with.

You may have one or more items in a category or you may have no items in a category. One of the things I have found that relieves stress is to make a list of all the things that are going on in my life positive or negative and how I can take action on them. Wow! I look at that list and think, "No wonder I was feeling anxious or uptight." The chart below is a more comprehensive way of doing it so that you know all aspects of what is going on in your life and can work through it to make sure there isn't a bigger issue. Sometimes we may be in a state of being healthy but still have stress. It's good to identify those stressors. For me, it takes their power away.

I have had some individuals ask me, "isn't that negative though, listing out all those things?" Well, if you choose to look at it as a negative, then that is what you will get out of the activity. If you choose a more proactive mindset and decide that you need to know both in order to take action to feel better, then it is perfect. When I make this list and see what all is on it, I have that "WOW" moment of clarity and understanding of why I was feeling the way I was. It allows me to not feel like I am just "making all this up" or that "something is wrong with me." I just recognize I do have a lot on my plate and now it is time to take action.

Let's get started on the Boundaries Inventory Graph activity. See the example provided.

Example:

Boundaries Inventory Graph

State of Being	External/ Internal	Action/ Inaction	Non-Accepting Behaviors	Belief	Action
Mental Negative self-talk	Internal	Inaction	Continue to make negative remarks about myself and allow others to as well	I'm not worthy	Read self-development books & work with a coach
Emotional					
Physical Car needs a new engine Gained 20lbs	External Internal	Action Inaction	None Continue to buy sugar products	None I am not pretty enough	Called auto repair shops Work with health coach & change beliefs
Spiritual Do not feel God loves or approves of me	Internal	Inaction	Avoid talking about spirituality	If you need God, you are weak	Talk to a spiritual counselor
Sexual					

Boundaries Inventory Graph

State of Being	External/ Internal	Action/ Inaction	Non-Accepting Behaviors	Belief	Action
Mental					
Emotional					
Physical					
Spiritual					
Sexual					

Boundaries or a lack of boundaries can show up in many areas of life. There is not a limit as to where boundaries can or cannot be set. It is important to take a look at each area of your life and examine if you have holes in your boundaries. Take a look at some of those areas:

- Financial
- Time
- Space
- Emotional
- Physical
- Spiritual

- Mental
- Sexual
- Food/Drink
- Low Self-Esteem
- Your own reality
- Needs/wants

Boundaries can be under utilized as well as over utilized. We often hear about individuals who put up walls. Walls - meaning they do not show much outward emotion to others, as well as setting strong physical boundaries. That may include not hugging, touching and/or seldom participating in events or social activities with others. This person may come off as "hard."

Putting up walls can be just as damaging as not setting enough boundaries. With walls, it is hard for a person to relax and enjoy their lives. They are often in the state of worry and mistrust. It is unfortunate, because they miss out on so much. The mistrust however is often a reaction to having been hurt in a previous situation. Individuals feel that if they just close themselves off from being hurt that they will be okay. However, I find more often than not, that the person is unhappier because of the walls. Again, like the previous activities, it is important to identify your behavior. Take a few minutes and write out areas where you are not setting boundaries and where you may be setting too many. I find that individuals primarily do one or the other. However, that is not always the case.

In what areas am I not setting boundaries?

1) _____

Reason: _____

Effects: _____

2) _____

Reason: _____

Effects: _____

3) _____

Reason: _____

Effects: _____

4) _____

Reason: _____

Effects: _____

5) _____

Reason: _____

Effects: _____

In what areas am I setting too many boundaries?

1) _____

Reason: _____

Effects: _____

2) _____

Reason: _____

Effects: _____

3) _____

Reason: _____

Effects: _____

4) _____

Reason: _____

Effects: _____

5) _____

Reason: _____

Effects: _____

One of the things to think about for those individuals that set too many boundaries because of fear of being hurt is to ask, "Is this real?" So much of the time we react based on the past and not on what is really happening right now. This is natural of course because no one wants to be set up for a repeat situation. However, we also have to be honest with ourselves and ask if we are being over protective or if the threat is real. It is like a parent who is over protective and doesn't allow their child to do things that others are allowed to. We become self-policing to the point of not living life.

In order to let go, we have to face what happened to us or how we were raised, and begin to change our philosophy. We have to go back and make the situation THEN accountable, not the current situation. For instance, we may have been badly hurt by a friend in college but if we penalize each person who comes into our path that is seeking friendship, then we are the ones who lose. It is unfair to that person, as well; that you are judging them on what someone else did to you. Of course, watch for signals in case you have a pattern of picking bad people or to be cautious, but it will be a lonely life if you make everyone responsible for something someone else did years ago.

Many times setting too hard of boundaries or "putting up walls" is a way individuals try to control their circumstances or not get emotionally hurt. When someone is doing this kind of behavior, they are essentially saying, "I am hurting" or, "I have been hurt and don't intend to open up and let it happen again." It is understandable, but usually doesn't work.

There is no excuse for controlling others' lives; however, it is understandable that we might exercise control over ours and others' lives out of a pattern of a dysfunctional upbringing. I never realized I was so controlling until one day I woke up and admitted my life wasn't working. I had to really listen to what people were saying and look at what they were doing to show me my controlling and dysfunctional behavior. I had to admit to myself that I came from a history of dysfunctional behavior and that now, I had to take responsibility for my actions as an adult.

I remember as a young girl, I would threaten my friends that if they did not come and play at my house with my toys that I would never play with them again. Sounds like normal child stuff; however, I usually won. I knew how to "direct, dominate, and command" them to do things the way I wanted. I learned early on and from the best. I felt that I was in control when I was on "my own turf". I felt I would be safer.

Have you ever noticed that in a lot of relationships, one person will be a quiet personality, almost submissive or needy and the other will be a more aggressive personality? I believe this is due to one person being a person without internal boundaries and the other without external boundaries. For the individual with no internal boundaries, they wouldn't have to make any decisions and therefore, wouldn't fail because it would be at the hands of someone else to blame; whereas, the more aggressive person may have control issues and find it easier to control a less aggressive individual. I have noticed children of dysfunctional families developing the personality of either category depending on their nature of survival.

It takes a lot of control to not control. Understand? Sometimes it takes a lot of effort to keep hands off of others' affairs. I really had to get that in my relationships. I would find myself asking my mate, "Have you done this? Have you done that?"

I would say, "Well, I do it because I love him so much." There came a time when I had to let go of the responsibility for everyone and let others do things for themselves. Anyway, they got along without me before we met, right? I would rationalize and think, "Not as well." I'm not saying that at times, partners can't remind each other of things, of course this is part of a partnership. I'm talking about the level at which it does become controlling.

I realized that as much as I wanted to, there were certain people in my life I just couldn't seem to stop controlling, even though I knew it wasn't my right. Those relationships either changed or they ended. Remember, you have a choice.

EXAMPLES OF CONTROLLING BEHAVIOR:

- Checking up on mates and children when unnecessary
- Tell someone they cannot do something or there will be unfavorable results (this could even be taken as an ultimatum)
- Giving advice and not letting go of an issue until the person takes the advice
- Not allowing someone to see certain friends or individuals because of your insecurities

Manipulation and control are very similar and can be hard to distinguish. I believe controlling is more forward, where manipulating is more underhanded. Neither is acceptable or functional if you are trying to take control of a person's affairs without their permission. It is my experience that individuals from dysfunctional families often do not really understand that they are either controlling or manipulating what goes on in their or others' lives. However, sometimes the person may be more sinister and may know what they are doing.

If I realized I was controlling and manipulating the relationship, it was certainly easy for me to justify that I was doing it in everyone's best interest. Imagine, now I could run others' lives better than they could, like I'd done such a great job of my own.

Do not underestimate children and their awareness level. One of the first recollections of being manipulative was when I was about four years old. My father was a traveling entertainer so he was seldom at home. When he did come home, a great deal of the time was spent drinking and fighting with my mother. I remember these loud arguments scared me tremendously.

One night, I was lying in bed and my parents had begun to fight again. I wanted them to stop fighting, so I consciously began to cry and entered the room in which they were arguing. My parents would stop arguing and tend to what they felt was taking care of my needs. They would "hush" me and send me back to bed. They were not capable of explaining to me why people fight or that it doesn't have anything to do with me. Yet somehow I had already been trained to come and "rescue" them. So, as I can recall, as early as four years old I was executing "dysfunctional behavior."

In self-development, we can discover we had dysfunctional behavior as small children. I believe children need to be made aware of why things occur. As an adult from a dysfunctional family, it was difficult to talk to children or other adults about things that made me feel uncomfortable. Topics such as anger, fear, death, sexual issues, and the list goes on. As we become adults, why does it become so uncomfortable to express our feelings and emotions? Maybe because this is how our parents expressed themselves to us. Yet again, it is in the behaviors that we learned.

As infants and children throughout our teenage years, we are totally dependent on our parents or caregivers to provide us with the things we need to survive: things such as food, clothing, and shelter. I know for me to maintain harmony, I felt a need to manipulate to keep receiving the things I needed to survive, since I was often threatened they might be taken away if I did not please my caregivers.

I have received a lot of peace and serenity from being honest with people since I have let go of my controlling and manipulating behavior. When I control or manipulate now, I recognize it immediately and then make amends, if possible. This is a very healing experience and takes time. You have the rest of your life, so why not live it honestly?

EXAMPLES OF MANIPULATING BEHAVIOR:

- To act or perform as if you are experiencing specific emotions or feelings to get a particular result.
- To not disclose honestly what you may be requesting from a person and allowing them to think differently.

Reasons People Don't Set Boundaries:

- Lack of understanding of own/others feelings
- Not having sufficient memory/data
- Personality development (learn from others, immaturity)
- Enmeshment (Father/God)
- Lack of understanding own needs/wants (martyr)
- No relationship with God (so others become that)
- Not wanting to face your feelings
- Abandonment fears
- Guilt & Shame
- FEAR
- Don't want to relive pain, doubt, etc…
  (I'll get into "trouble")

When we first meet someone, it is easy to get swept up in the excitement of having someone pay attention to us. It may be easy to overlook obvious things that would indicate an unhealthy relationship. These guidelines can help in setting boundaries and deciding to pursue a relationship with an individual or not. Here is an example of how you can turn these statements into a guideline of questions:

1) Does he/she share feelings?
2) Does he/she speak honestly and straight forward?
3) Does he/she nurture me?
4) Does he/she listen to my needs and wants?
5) Do they respect my physical boundaries?
   Etc…

Here are some quick tips to setting more simple boundaries:

- Have values and help others to understand them
- Set goals and priorities
- Create a schedule so you know when you have extra time
- Use language like: "Let me check my calendar and get back to you"
- Understand your needs, wants, thoughts and feelings from others needs, wants, thoughts and feelings
- Avoid situations or people where you know you may be uncomfortable
- Get assistance to help you change your self-talk

When you are setting healthy boundaries,
you are RESPECTING yourself!!

Remembering MY Boundaries

One of the ways to become good with setting boundaries in your life and changing your behavior is to become hyper aware of your behavior. I like to give this simple assignment to my clients as a way to make them aware. I want you to write a list of the things you GIVE UP when you DO NOT set boundaries.

You see, when we don't set boundaries, we are either giving our "gifts" away or allowing someone to take them from you. I also consider these items to be your "goal" that is used in the previous "tree" activity. As you look at the list, think about these things. These are things that we desire and want to obtain…our goals.

Here is an example so you understand:

When I don't set this boundary:	**I give up:**
Don't say "no" to an activity	Energy
Don't tell someone not to talk to me negatively	Respect
Enter a relationship just to have attention	Love
Spend years with people who don't respect me	Time
I act as a "human doing"	Peace

You get the example. I feel that God gives us gifts that He WANTS us to have, that we deserve. We deserve to have peace in our life, energy and respect among other things. What are you compromising by not setting boundaries? Here is a list of things you may be giving up or allowing others to take from you because of not setting boundaries.

Energy
Respect
Love
Time
Peace
Passion
Self-Esteem
Dignity

Friendship
Patience
Dreams
Money
Security
Integrity
Independence
Health

Now write how you don't set boundaries and what you are giving away because of it:

When I don't set this boundary: **I give up:**

_____   _____

_____   _____

_____   _____

_____   _____

_____   _____

_____   _____

_____   _____

_____   _____

Now for the fun activity. I want you to make a necklace, bracelet or some other piece of art that will remind you of your "gifts." For instance, if you decide on a bracelet, I want you to have a charm for each "gift" you discovered that you find that you tend to give away. As you are in your "hyper-aware" mode of your behavior, if you find that you have just put yourself in a situation where you either "gave away" a gift or allowed someone to "take it from you," I want you to remove the charm that represents the "gift" you just gave away. Keep it off for the day (or an hour) and then put it back on. This is an activity to make you accurately aware that you allowed something to happen. This activity isn't to chastise you, it is to make you more aware and make you WANT to keep your charms (gifts). It keeps us in check with our behavior.

So, what do you want your "charms/gifts" to be?

Charm #1_____

Charm #2 _____

Charm #3_____

Charm #4 _____

Charm #5 _____

Charm #6 _____

Charm #7 _____

Charm #8 _____

Charm #9 _____

Charm #10_____

Behaviors That Keep Us In dysfunction:

To begin taking responsibility for my life, I had to first look at the dysfunction that I grew up around. In the next pages, I have presented common behaviors or issues of our caregivers that might have been passed along to us. It is amazing how we grow up with behaviors that we accept as okay or even normal. The sad situation is that I notice many parents or peers ignoring signals from their child's behavior that something may be seriously wrong. Maybe they are too afraid to look at the possibility that they had something to do with their child's behavioral problems. I just can't accept that as an excuse. Remember, these "behaviors" are often times a lack boundaries. They go hand in hand.

When I was about five years old, I had an imaginary friend. We have all heard this is normal; however, I believe my imaginary friend was representing a lot more than just the need for a companion. My friend did not have a name, per se. I called him my "red, purple and orange boyfriend." I really didn't understand at first why I called him this until I got into the self-development process.

You see, when I talked to other people about my "red, purple and orange boyfriend," I would tell them how we would get into fights. Then, I would go on to explain how I killed my boyfriend. I would explain how I either stabbed him, shot him, or beat him up. The thing that gets me now is, why didn't my parents, siblings, or babysitter question why I might have such a violent imagination and need for revenge? Through self-development, I now understand my "red, purple and orange boyfriend" was a mirror of my father. It is interesting how things will come out in a child. I think the colors represented my anger towards my father. I was lucky; I became aware and didn't have a violent tendency. We can't say that for everyone unfortunately.

My caregivers did not even realize there was a problem with me because of their own denial. They felt that I had it easier or better than they had it, so they didn't look closely at what was going on with me. The problem lies in my caregivers who hadn't resolved issues of their past and therefore, were still carrying around the dysfunctional behaviors and passing it along to me.

My mother was an alcoholic. She stopped drinking when she was in her forties, only to start taking tranquilizers. She never received any counseling. She still continued to live in fear, sadness, anger, and many other feelings that drowned her happiness and choice for life. She was too fearful to look at her past. She kept her feelings within her, and as a result, she led a life of much illness. My experience has shown me that if you are not expressing your feelings, they will find somewhere else to go: in my opinion, usually internally. I feel this is where illness begins. For so many years, I thought my mother was in control. For so many years, I thought I was in control. I think there were too many chiefs and not enough Indians. In the end, this all represented a lack of boundaries; which in turn, became these behaviors.

There are many types of dysfunctional behaviors due to abuse or poorly learned beliefs and behavior. Now is the time to make a choice as to if you want to overcome them and how you want to live. Let's take a look at what may be holding you back:

FEAR

There are two ways of looking at fear. One is that fear often holds us back from doing things we would like to do. The other being that fear can catapult you into becoming willing and deciding to take action to make changes. You can either let fear keep control over you or let fear move you in a positive direction to overcome it. Fear can keep you safe from harm and can help you learn what it takes to survive.

When starting my self-development program, I first asked myself, "What am I fearful of?" Then, I asked myself, "What is the worst thing that could happen? How would I let this affect me? Is it worth it?" I knew for myself things really couldn't get much worse. I was already so numb that I couldn't feel anything. It was definitely worth it to me to try something new so that I could have a chance at living life fully. Even if it meant that I might lose everything around me that was familiar. I didn't have anything to lose, because my spirit was already dead, and I probably would be too, if something didn't change.

I'm sure you've probably heard the expression, "All you have to fear is fear itself," said by President Franklin Delano Roosevelt in a speech. This is really true. Take away fear, and you have many doors of opportunities. If someone conditions you to believe how bad carrots taste and then you are presented with carrots to eat, there is probably a certain amount of fear and hesitation you might experience before you began eating them. Then you hesitantly eat one and realize they aren't so bad and the more you eat the more you grow to like them. Carrots aren't really such scary things; however, many things in a child's life that makes us fearful carry through to us as adults.

My mother was so deep in her fear; she would complain that she did not want to live. She told us that if she had the guts to kill herself she would. Talk about a double dose of fear. My sister, who was about sixteen at the time, had about all she could take. One day my mother was deep in her misery and making more death wishes. My sister picked up my mother's gun, handed it to my mother and told her that if she really didn't want to live, then to go ahead and kill herself. My mother had placed my sister in a position that was not appropriate. It was not my sister's responsibility to be the parent; yet, my mother was too fearful to grow up and make mature decisions.

Fifteen years later, my mother was still making these sorts of comments. I cannot tell you how many times I reached out to her and tried to help. She was too fearful. She never took my advice or if she did seek help, it would be very short lived. I finally got to the point where I was also telling my mother that if she wanted to end her life, then that decision was strictly up to her and I would not feel guilty for her doing so. We can only do so much for others. The only person we can really take care of is ourselves. Please understand, I LOVED my mother. However, I had to love myself more in order to survive.

It is not surprising that my mother had suicidal tendencies. Her mother tried to commit suicide twice. Both times my mother found her. The first time my mother was about seven. She told me the story of how she was playing with her cousins when she all of a sudden she had a bad feeling and was compelled to locate her mother. She asked around, and no one had seen her mother. She was told by her family to relax, that maybe her mother had taken a walk. My mother kept searching and eventually found my grandmother hanging in the attic with a rope around her neck. She was able to call her father for help in enough time to save her mother's life. Grandma promised her that she would never try to commit suicide again. Approximately seven years later, she broke that promise.

When my mother was about fourteen, my grandmother, still baring the neck scar from her first suicide attempt, took an overdose. Once again, my mother found her and was able to call for help in time. My mother used this as an excuse as to why she would never commit suicide. She didn't want to hurt us. She wasn't even concerned with herself. She just remembered her mother's broken promises.

Fear usually always has to do with change. As we discussed previously, people have a tendency to resist or be reluctant to change. Fear gives us a bigger excuse not to change. This is the time to make it work, to make a change. Look fear in the eye and call its bluff. You are a strong person. You can set your mind to do whatever you want. Do not let other people's fear stand in the way of what you want for yourself. We each need to make decisions for ourselves.

WHAT FEAR HOLDS YOU BACK FROM OBTAINING:

- Having a satisfying relationship
- Holding the job or career you desire
- The ability to accept change
- Positive growth
- Financial stability
- Friends and family of choice

If fear was not holding you back, what would you be doing/accomplishing?

1) _____

2) _____

3) _____

4) _____

5) _____

ILLUSIONS/DENIAL

All of my life, the events that happened have just seemed like stories. I always felt somewhat detached and in denial about how bad things were. I had many illusions about my upbringing, my parents and my siblings. Some of it was because of denial and some of it was what others wanted me to see.

We all like to think that things are great and perfect. Yet, what we feel inside tells us differently. When I would be going through a lot of emotions, I would sometimes think that I was out of touch with myself. Later, I learned just the opposite was true. When you are going through and feeling your emotions, you are in touch with yourself.

When you feel your emotions and allow yourself to be honest within your body, you will find the truth comes to the surface. It is painful to relive events; however, until I had an understanding of what happened, it was difficult to start the process of letting go. Self-development is a life-long proposition. It doesn't mean staying in the pain your entire life. It means being aware of yourself and moving out of the pain and moving on.

When I was in a drawing class, my teacher told us that the one thing that his students are the most afraid of when drawing, is to use their eraser and start over or fix something they did not like. He told us to not be afraid of our eraser. Pick up your eraser; because your life can look anyway you want it to. If it is not what you imagine, then change it.

Maybe you are in a relationship now and are experiencing difficulty with intimacy because of unresolved abuse and abandonment issues. Or maybe you are still experiencing pain about someone harming you. You are frightened to become close with someone because of these past events. But by not dealing with these things you stay in denial which prevents you from obtaining the gifts that God has for you.

Being conscious of life can be difficult for those individuals dealing with a lot of painful memories. I believe there are two levels of consciousness. The first level of consciousness is being aware you came from a family with problems; however, you deny the full impact it is having on your life and don't make changes. The second level being that you are totally aware and conscious of the dysfunction and understand you have a lot of emotions about what happened to you, realizing there are issues to be dealt with and taking action. Denial comes in at the first level of consciousness where people are usually too fearful to dig any deeper about themselves and their emotions. Some individuals may never face their realities of childhood on any conscious level. Remember to ask yourself, would you rather be in short term pain to fix the problem or long term unhappiness?

What are you still in denial about?

1) _____

How does it hold you back?

_____

2) _____

How does it hold you back?

_____

3) _____

How does it hold you back?

_____

4) _____

How does it hold you back?

_____

5) _____

How does it hold you back?

_____

WORTHLESSNESS

While my father was traveling, he accepted a position for a short time at a hotel as the manager and entertainer. My mother, sister, and I went to go visit him for several days. I was about five. During our stay, one of the hotel floors caught fire. Everyone had to be evacuated immediately. We had been in the bar watching my father perform when the news broke about the fire. We were told to go outside, across from the hotel. My sister and I were still wearing our pajamas. This was in Indiana on New Years' Eve and the weather was extremely cold. We were freezing cold.

There were two beautiful women with fur coats who offered them to my mother to keep us warm. My mother was holding me and so one of the ladies draped the coat around me. After a few minutes my father came out to let us know what was taking place. He saw the coats and the women standing beside us. He made us take off the coats and give them back to the ladies. We were back to freezing in our little pajamas. I felt like I was unworthy of being properly taken care of. It felt as if he cared about those women more than me. I know if I had a small child in the cold weather, I would accept the assistance from the ladies. I'll never know what motivated my father to take this action; however, I do know how it made me feel. This is how behaviorally people can SHOW us our worth. It was he who was wrong though, not my worth. God made me worthy at birth.

We all want to feel valuable to others, especially our parents. It is just human. However, the most important thing is feeling valuable to yourself. Treat yourself with care and love. As parents, show children how to develop love and healthy pride for themselves. Show children they are worthy through your actions and words. To develop your self-worth, give yourself love and attention. If self-worth was not taught to you as a child, then this is the time to instill a new belief of worthiness about yourself. Start by imagining the little girl or boy you once were. Now imagine your adult self talking to your little child self and saying that she or he is a precious child worthy of all the love in the world. Trouble begins when we don't take care of ourselves.

When I wasn't feeling worthy, I felt like I had to live up to the expectations of others. This is often where perfection behavior begins. I wasn't given the awareness of self-esteem and self-worth. I had nothing to live for except others. Worth was based on your looks, your job, and your wallet in my family. My father judged my sister-in-law immediately because she came from Kentucky, was thin, and didn't have perfect teeth. When my teeth came in somewhat imperfect as a possible result of my mother's negligence, I experienced a lot of distress. I imagined my father abandoning me further because of the condition of my teeth. In the eighth grade, I had my teeth bonded to make them look better. From then on I blessed all dentists until I gained self-esteem.

Ways I am worthy:

_____   _____

_____   _____

_____   _____

_____   _____

_____   _____

BURDEN

Parents have a choice whether they want a child or not. It is too bad that once a parent decides to either have a child or keep a child that they cannot accept their decision. In my experience, expressing either verbally or physically that a child is a burden is not accepting the decision. Expressing the feelings of being burdened is devastating to a child that primarily wants love and attention. Sitting in Adult Children of Alcoholics meetings, I've heard countless stories of individuals' feelings about being a burden. In some way or another, I believe that adults brought up in dysfunction usually feel they were a burden to their parents.

Maybe your parents expressed how they had to sacrifice to provide you with things or that money was tight because of the extra mouth to feed. How could a child feel they were not a burden by these types of things being said to them? My experience is that there are usually a lot of different ways our parents made us feel like a burden.

My mother always commented that if it weren't for having children, she would still be on the entertainment circuit with her singing career. My mother was very talented and she had a record deal presented to her. However, they were not interested in my father's music abilities. My father could be a very jealous man. Fear of him leaving her and having a child kept her from going for it and accepting the record deal. My mother used things in her life as an excuse because of her fear, and as a result, she lost out on many wonderful opportunities like this one.

Nothing is a burden if you take that approach: even bills. Love your bills because without them you wouldn't have a lot of the things in life that you enjoy. They also teach you responsibility. And someone is being nice to you for extending you credit.

If you grew up with the message that you were a burden, it is time to recognize that instead, you are a gift from God. Your personality is unique and you ARE here for a reason!

How was I TOLD I was a burden?

_____

_____

_____

How was I SHOWN I was a burden?

_____

_____

_____

FAILURE

If parents use the word "failure" to describe their child in front of them, they are being verbally abusive, controlling, and manipulative. Who are we to say anyone is a failure and what a cruel thing to say about a child. Maybe you heard statements like: "You are a failure. You will never amount to anything." Making a statement like this is setting an individual up for failure and low self-esteem.

As a child growing up, you probably spent most, or at least half, of your time around your parents. For me, it was easy to assume that my caregivers knew best since they had so much time to observe me. After time and enough put-downs, it's hard not to take on the beliefs of their words or behaviors.

I was about nine years old when I was on a local swim team. My father was in town and came to watch one of my swim practices. We were participating in relay races preparing for an upcoming race. I was so nervous about him being there and felt I could never live up to his expectations. I hardly ever saw him, and it was important for me to make a good impression. During conversations with him on the phone, he would put down my siblings and other family members for the way they did things. So, obviously, I got the message that I couldn't fail. Otherwise, he would talk down about me and potentially not love me.

My nerves and fear got the best of me. After lagging behind the other swimmers in the race, I quit early and complained of a bad stomach ache. I apologized to my father for letting him down. He told me he understood, and I was let off the hook. I felt like such a failure because I had made up an excuse of a stomach ache to get out of performing. I'd rather make the excuse of a stomach ache than come in last during the race.

When I started self-development, I had to erase all of the old negative data that I received about myself as well as the belief about failure. No one is a failure. We may choose circumstances that do not work out for us in the end; however, every situation yields an important lesson that is priceless. If we are caught up in fear and others' ideas of who we are, then we cannot accept these situations as a lesson.

If I said my marriage was a failure because I divorced, then I wouldn't be seeing the larger picture. Without my first marriage, who knows what kind of situation I would be in now. I am very grateful for the experience I have had to be able to wake up into consciousness. Turn your "failures" into successes. It is all in the way we look at it. Situations can fail but YOU are not a failure. Failure allows us to learn and get to what is really the right answer in our life or situation. Failure IS a mindset!

Oath of Success!

I,_____, CHOOSE to look at my failures as opportunities for change and discovery. I look at them as a positive and will allow them to better me.

Signed_____Date_____

FEAR OF ABANDONMENT

Throughout my life, I have felt there is a sign on my forehead saying "STAY AWAY." I had a father who wasn't around much and other family members that both physically and emotionally abandoned me. Abandonment is especially hard on a child who doesn't understand. Children are so innocent, yet take blame so easily. Unfortunately, a child may think a parent has left because they were "bad." And more unfortunate is that parents often can't or won't express and communicate the real causes of abandonment, which leaves the child with this belief. An adult may not understand why their mate or family member left. However, children as well as adults need reassuring that they are not in any way at fault.

I pulled into an auto center, and there was a van slowly driving away. I was waiting on this van so that I could pull into a parking space. I wondered why they were driving so slowly. Then I noticed that there was a little girl standing quite a distance from the van. She was probably about three years old and she was crying frantically with her arms raised in the air in the direction of the van.

My heart dropped, wondering if this little girl belonged to the people in the van. Finally, the van stopped as the little girl's screams became louder. Her father got out of the van, went and picked her up in an uncaring and scolding manner, and began yelling at her for being "bad." Apparently, he was trying to teach her a lesson that they were going to leave her behind if she didn't "straighten up." I became furious at what I had just witnessed. This is not the way to teach a child anything.

When you have been abandoned by someone close to you at an early age, it may be difficult as an adult to trust others, even if it is just a threat of abandonment. This may draw you towards emotionally shallow relationships as an adult. If a parent expressed to you that the people you love will always leave you, it is likely you may select people who will carry out this behavior. We don't choose these people consciously. But we do choose them out of what we know.

I had only been married one day when my first husband said he thought he had made a wrong decision. He said it wasn't me-- even that he loved me. He told me that he was scared of commitment and found it best to go back to his home town. Being the great manipulator that I was, I managed to talk him out of it. If only I'd known.

He stuck around for about a month and was having difficulty finding or keeping a job. I was financially supporting the both of us. Then, one day, I came home and the closets were cleaned out. Everything of his was gone. My heart fell to the ground and I can still remember the absolute terror of him leaving me. We had moved to this town about a month before we got married so that I could accept a manager's position with the company I was working for. I knew no one except my employees. I was devastated, ashamed, and felt desperate.

There is a certain insight we all have that I can't explain. My husband had briefly mentioned joining the service. That had been some time before; however, as soon as I read my "Dear Jane" letter explaining his departure, I started calling local recruiters. How I knew, I'll never know, except that it was a gift of discernment from God. Sure enough he had joined a branch of the service and was off to go through the military entry processing center.

I called the bus station and had him paged. He had just gotten off the bus and was almost out of the door when he heard his name being called. He picked up the phone and to his surprise, I was on the other end. I begged and pleaded until he eventually came back home; however, he still insisted on joining the service. He went into the service and the night after his graduation, he ended up going AWOL.

Before my husband quit the service, he and his recruiter had talked me into joining the service; however, I legally got out of my obligations to serve because of the stress I was under. We were both so co-dependent that we couldn't be apart while he was in the service. I'm sure the armed services was glad to get rid of this needy and frantic girl that I had suddenly become.

After he went AWOL, we went to my mother's house in Kentucky to stay for a few weeks until we could get a place of our own. She would not let us stay at her house because of the conflicts between the family and me and my husband, so we returned to Dallas. At the time, she was heavy into taking tranquilizers and the lies she was telling were mounting. I was feeling abandoned by my mother and confused about my relationship with my husband.

My husband promised me he would talk to me before ever making any hasty decisions again. He broke that promise about five months later when we woke up one morning and he just announced he had found an apartment and would be gone by day's end. I had no time to do anything because I had to get to work. It took two days, and we were back together. He seemed to understand, and even explained to me his fear of commitment. He was a victim of emotional abandonment himself. I believe it was easier for him to not deal with me or others.

Out of that relationship, as painful as it was, I learned important lessons that are a part of my being able to write this book. For that, I am very grateful. Interestingly, my husband had become very committed to our relationship the second time I took him back. However, I think my cup was over flowing and a couple of years later we decided to divorce. I had finally become conscious of what I was drawing into my life and was starting to clean up my situations. For many years my first husband and I remained friends helping each other in various ways. Shockingly, as I write this book, I am grieving the fact that last week, after 22 years, I had to tell him to never contact me again.

Apparently what I didn't know was during those first times of him leaving me, he had been communicating with an ex-girlfriend. She was frantically trying to win him over, even calling the Army Base where he was stationed. She contacted me through a social media outlet and told me she had been "watching" me for the last three months and that she had wanted to apologize to my ex-husband for how she had treated him. She was hoping to get his phone number from me. Unbelievable!

She confessed many things to me about her and my first husband's relationship that I knew nothing about.

I imagine a great part of his leaving me both times was around his confusion between the two relationships. I had NO CLUE of another woman except that during those few months I acted like the neediest, most pathetic person imaginable. Yes, I had abandonment issues, but I had never acted this fearful and out of control. Now that I understand God's gifts of discernment and prophecy over my life, I can clearly see now that instinctually, I KNEW! Now I understand I just didn't have the facts, which was driving me to much anxiousness and inappropriate behavior. I believe we all really need to get in tune with our personal discernment and LISTEN to what it tells you. DO NOT ignore it or think you are "crazy". Now I realize I was crazy for not listening to what God was telling me. He has these gifts for ALL of us!

I had remained friends to my first husband for the past 22 years and I can't believe, at no time, did he consider telling me the truth. We were married and he chose to keep this lie. Then we became friends and still held on to the lie, knowing that maybe this information would help me to process some things. It tells me how selfish he continues to be to this day. He never was one for taking responsibility. I reached out to him to get 3 questions answered. I felt like these answers would truly help me piece together some of my past. I waited a week after the woman contacted me and carefully thought as to whether it was best to reach out to him and share this revelation. The "other woman" reached out to ease her shame and guilt that she had carried for 22 years. This is a fact she confessed to me. In the end and by my putting my "coaching hat" on, she realized she really didn't need to apologize to me (which she did) or my first husband. She needed to apologize and forgive herself for her own behavior and dysfunction.

Unfortunately, my ex-husband did the selfish routine and refused to answer my questions. At no time did I say, "How dare you?" or "How could you have done this to me?" I have not had feelings for this man for years and blaming him was not my agenda. My point in contacting him was to have three important questions answered that would resolve within me a much needed answer. But at no point would he take any responsibility. He even tried turning it on me. This was when I decided to end this relationship. For what I thought was a long standing friendship, I am now grieving.

Someone I talked to even said to me, "Why ask these questions after 22 years…why not just go on with life." I could have done that but these were important to understanding my actions as well as lessons I can take forward. Being that I was the one inappropriately contacted by this woman, I did not ask or start this explosion in my life. I now needed something resolved that I had not known before. I deserved to have those three questions answered! At no time did I impose blame his way. That, I knew, I did not need to do.

Here's what I have to say about the "why ask after 22 years"…Just because it's been 22 year does not make him "not a liar." He is still a liar and a deceiver. Time DOES NOT justify wrongs. If you murder someone 10 years ago, you should (a healthy should) still pay. I wasn't asking my ex to pay. I was simply asking him to HELP ME understand MY behavior by answering these three questions. And, the questions were so easy, but, he would have had to admit the truth, which he refused to do. He gave me his answer by not answering!

From my personal experience, emotional abandonment is when an individual is unable to communicate his or her feelings, shuts down to others' feelings, and ignores or denies situations. All of this can lead a person to physical abandonment. My mother gave me the message that all men will eventually hurt and leave you because it is what my father did to her as well as his children. I now develop healthier relationships with others because of the many years of self-development work I chose to work though.

As adults now, we first have to not abandon ourselves any more. If you are in avoidance or denial, you are abandoning yourself.

It is hard to understand how someone can abandon either emotionally or physically, but we have to come to terms with not understanding. Sometimes we may be dealing with a narcissist, sociopath or some other mentally challenged type of person that CANNOT be there and will do the abandoning.

My father was clearly a sociopath, though as a child and young woman I didn't want to believe it. Years later, through self-education and after much healing, I now see the situation for what it was. Again, when you are dealing with someone that cannot either mentally or emotionally be there for you, it is NOT about you. Though they are hurting you, I feel like it is a sickness. My husband kept leaving me because of his emotional instability. My father abandoned me because of his mental instability. There is a difference and it is good to know. There is much healing in understanding. In both cases, it wasn't about me. My "picker" was off because of my belief system and this is why I chose my first husband. I believed I wasn't worthy and so guess what I picked!

Who or how was I abandoned?

1) _____

How does it hold you back?

_____

2) _____

How does it hold you back?

_____

3) _____

How does it hold you back?

_____

4) _____

How does it hold you back?

_____

5) _____

How does it hold you back?

_____

ISOLATING

Through talking to others in similar circumstances I have discovered that isolation is common in adults of dysfunctional families and especially in those individuals that have experienced abandonment. As children, we learned it was not usually safe being around others, and so it was easier to isolate from friends than have the possibility of being hurt.

For me, being alone meant not having to be subjected to judgment, criticism, and the possibility of abandonment. However, isolation often means being unfulfilled and lonely. It takes a strong commitment to take a step in making friends and having relationships. You have to overcome fear and release yourself from your past.

Neglect from parents and family also can cause isolation. When a person is neglected physically and emotionally, they are already used to being alone, and so isolating themselves is a learned response. Sadly, what I've seen is that parents neglect their children sometimes because they themselves came from dysfunctional families with neglect, and they never learned how to overcome the behavior and function well with others.

As parents, it is important to spend time with your child. Give children an opportunity to express their emotions. Children learn directly from their parents. If children see their parents involved with friends and social activities, it is likely they will learn to function well among others. If a parent does not have friends and seldom leaves the house, it is likely the child will grow up to do the same. To begin putting an end to the isolation, you have to take initiative to try new things. No one is going to show up at your door and drag you out of your isolation. We just have to risk a little and get ourselves out there among others.

How Do I Isolate Myself?

1) _____

2) _____

3) _____

4) _____

5) _____

What are things I would like to be doing?

1) _____

2) _____

3) _____

4) _____

5) _____

FROZEN FEELINGS

I think the major thing that helped me to decide to start self-development was the fact that I could no longer feel anything. I couldn't feel love for myself, others, or work. I wasn't motivated towards anything, nor could I see my future in sight. I had frozen feelings and unless I did something to thaw, I would eventually break. It is amazing the amount of stress our bodies can handle.

Giving up your wants and needs (gifts) can lead you to frozen feelings. If we are giving up everything to someone else, how can we have anything left for ourselves? It is time you give back to yourself. We deserve to have our wants and needs fulfilled. I realize it is hard after a lifetime to all of a sudden decide not to take anymore, and start listening to your needs. We have to do everything on a gradual basis.

Start taking time out for yourself. Begin by setting boundaries with individuals about what you are capable and willing to do. Listen to what your body is telling you, and let your feelings flow. It is okay to cry, get angry, or yell. These types of things can often be repressed in children of dysfunctional families. God gave you tears, a temper, and a loud voice, so if you feel you want to express an emotion, by all means release it: appropriately, of course. I'm not saying go off on someone, these are things we can do by ourselves. However, we have to get our emotions out to get unstuck!

I've noticed many individuals are held back by shame. Feelings are nothing to be ashamed of. This is why I have you do the "tree" activity. This activity starts to identify the feelings surrounding the internal negative belief you have. It is hard to face, it is overwhelming and this is where we get stuck. It is crucial that you work through the tree activity for each negative belief you have about yourself. You deserve to feel positive emotions! You deserve to be happy!

Activity:
Go through the feeling/behavior list and circle the words that you believe you are frozen to. Select one word a day and journal about that word and what it means to you. If you need clarity on the word/feeling, look it up in the dictionary. Journaling about feelings helps us to open up and begin to feel again. When you journal, ask about that word the: what, when, where, who, and how questions. You can write about stories as well as family member experiences. I will write more about journaling later in this book.

INTIMACY

Adult children of dysfunction often have problems being intimate with others. It is not surprising considering the atmosphere you might have grown up around. I feel there are several concepts of intimacy. Some people only refer to intimacy as having sex. Intimacy also means expressing yourself and your emotions by communicating with someone else. Some will have difficulty with intimacy in all areas.

Trust is a large factor in intimacy. There are many ways to be intimate. I would imagine that sexual abuse victims probably have the hardest time feeling comfortable with intimacy. The trust has been betrayed by individuals they may have been originally comfortable with and had trusted initially.

To open up and share yourself, there has to be trust in the relationship. For a dysfunctional family, this is totally foreign. There is no familiarity with intimacy because it never happened. It is very important to first and foremost develop an intimate relationship with yourself. How can you share yourself with someone else if you don't understand yourself? With the proper tools, anyone can learn to become comfortable with intimacy.

When you are co-dependent, it is not likely you are going to understand your own deepest nature. Instead, your concerns are with the person you are care taking. Listen to your needs, wants, hopes, and dreams. Find out what is important to you and your values. Do not focus on what your family told you about these things. How do you think and feel about things? You may not know, so you may have to start trying things out to be able to determine that.

Being intimate starts with getting to know yourself. Trust yourself first and then, if you choose, share your feelings with someone you trust. You always have a choice in everything you do. Feeling comfortable with intimacy takes time and nurturing.

Who do I avoid my feelings with?

_____

_____

_____

_____

SABOTAGE

It is hard to think that we would purposely, knowingly, or even unconsciously try to sabotage ourselves and our success. Yet often as children of dysfunction, we do just that. Given the messages of being unworthy, unlovable, and so on, we may believe we don't deserve to have success. I believe we attract situations that might prevent us from fulfilling goals or dreams.

I had a friend who was an athlete. Every year he seemed to turn out the same. He would train hard and then something, usually illness, would come up and prevent him from that "big race." He had a fear of success. His family had taught him through words and actions that he was a failure. I believe that in his mind, that was what he thought of himself. Every year he proved his family right. The unconscious belief is that if you continue to fail or sabotage success, then you won't have to try to meet the expectations of success, and in actuality, you are meeting the expectations of your family. As adults, it becomes very hard to undo all of those messages. It takes awareness, perseverance, courage, and faith.

Self-development is just that…development of yourself. It takes time and no one is perfect. You may slip every once in a while; however, I believe there is always a major lesson in the experience that maybe you haven't gotten yet. Remember, it is okay to make a mistake. Without the experiences I have had, I wouldn't be where I am now.

For years I sabotaged my personal and romantic relationships through lack of communication, fear of intimacy, being judgmental and other behaviors that kept me from being close to someone. I sabotaged my relationships unconsciously in the past because I didn't believe I deserved a great, healthy relationship and partner. I had a lot of fear, mostly of abandonment. So essentially, I would unconsciously set up a situation of sabotage because of my "old tapes" that made me feel as if it were eventually going to happen anyway. This was a "mental tape" that would run when my self-esteem was low. I've now replaced it with a tape that says, "I am deserving of the best. I deserve to have a healthy relationship and partner. I love and accept myself just as I am."

Again, you are seeing the theme of how beliefs are so intrinsic to our success. Years ago, I personally worked through most all of my old negative beliefs, then, only a few years ago, I discovered that I had not fully worked through one of them. That was the belief that I deserved career success.

My second husband and I worked for the same company and we found ourselves coming home each night only to plop down on the couch and watch hours of television. In between the show at commercial time or at dinner we would often gripe about how we weren't living our dream or making enough money or...blah, blah, blah. You get the point. This was the first four years of our relationship. Because my husband had this same internal negative belief on board himself, we perpetuated each other's behavior. For years we talked about "when, if only, one day." We finally got sick of hearing ourselves talk and one day "woke up" and realized this negative talk and figured out we still had something we had to work through. Once that realization happened for my husband and me, along with being sick of hearing ourselves talk, it was our golden ticket out of complacency.

Shortly after this realization, my husband got a Director's position and a 35% pay increase, and I started my own company that I now successfully run. These were all pipe dreams before because of our internal belief about success. This is why it is SO important to make sure you check every nook and cranny and turn every stone over making sure you have revealed ALL of your old negative beliefs in order to deal with them. A higher level of success is in store for you! You just have to believe it and then take action!

What do I want to stop sabotaging?

1) _____

What will I have to do differently?

_____

2) _____

What will I have to do differently?

_____

3) _____

What will I have to do differently?

_____

4) _____

What will I have to do differently?

_____

5) _____

What will I have to do differently?

_____

OVERACHIEVERS

We just got through looking at sabotage in which individuals may consciously set up situations that prevent them from success. Now, we're going to look at individuals who over strive to be recognized as a success by others. It is great to be aggressive and go after our goals. We all want success. However, what price will you pay for success? At what point will you consider yourself a success? Setting goals is a great way to achieve what you want. Are your goals and wants reasonable?

I've known individuals who work themselves so hard, trying to be better and better to show their parents that they are successful. They lose sight of friends, relationships, and other needs and wants. The overachiever is trying to meet their parents or other's expectations. Just like when dealing with sabotage, we must again look at expectations. We can spend a lifetime proving ourselves to others, and what does it do for us? It usually leaves us with more feelings of emptiness, unworthiness, and feelings of being non-deserving when we don't get that big pat on the back we were striving for.

It is hard to believe that we may never be acceptable by another person's standards. However, letting go of this need to be accepted is essential to our happiness. If you accept that you do not have to meet other's expectations, it becomes easier to accept yourself for who you are. Of course, I'm not saying that in a healthy relationship that you throw caution to the wind. There are healthy levels of expectation but you have to accept yourself to have true acceptance from others.

Remember that your parents may not know how to be close to you, and so they may use expectations to keep you at arms' length. This is about them, not about you. They may be as fearful as you are. Just because they are parents doesn't mean they are super-human, all-knowing individuals.

We are all doing the best we can in this time and space. We have to love and accept ourselves. Without this, we usually go back to square one. We will have the same situations over and over until we learn what it is that we don't seem to understand. Be easy with yourself. Would you expect so much out of a friend or a family member? So why expect so much out of yourself?

CO-DEPENDENCY

The following is the way I understand co-dependency. Co-dependents need people in their life to affirm their existence, their beliefs, and their love. Co-dependents usually have low self-esteem and have difficulty loving and accepting themselves. They search for someone who will affirm these feelings for them. However, at the same time, many co-dependents are also care-takers themselves; being persons who fulfill the functions for those who may not be capable or they allow the caretaker to take over their decisions.

Co-dependents will give up their own wants and needs to fulfill the wants and needs of others. This action will make a person feel noble and needed. Remember, a co-dependent person looks to others for their feelings of worthiness. Co-dependents are often martyrs and will make you think they are independent and strong. They are often in a dance of manipulation and control.

I believe individuals are set up to be co-dependent before they realize it. The way I was brought up often dictated my patterns until I made a conscious effort to change. My entire family was co-dependent, everyone dabbling in everyone else's affairs except their own, sometimes having to for survival.

At the age of two, I became very ill with a very high temperature. My mother was passed out cold from having drunk too much again. My sister was eight years old. She would take care of me during instances like this. This particular time, my fever got so high that my sister bathed me in cool water, rubbed me down, and fed me ice pops. She got the temperature to finally go down without help from my mother. Without my sister, I might have had severe complications or even died.

I, like my siblings, was placed in a parental role at a time when I needed my parents and other children to play with. Instead, I learned how to take care of others and did not receive a healthy sense of self. I often hear parents tell young children that this is "the real world." Why take away a precious time in an individual's life? Children will learn about the world and responsibility soon enough. Young children don't need to be burdened with the role of being parent, spouse, and caretaker. If you are a parent and find yourself in a dilemma, reach out to another parent, friend, counselor, or anyone else other than your child to help you through problems. Ask for guidance from God to direct you towards a positive, healthy life.

Co-dependency is a way for people to avoid their own lives. These individuals will often get caught up in drama in other peoples' lives or even create drama in their own life to receive "affirmation" that they are worthy. See, if I "fix" this situation, they will allow me to "stick around." I will have "earned" my place. You see where this thinking and behavior becomes toxic and overwhelming. Co-dependency runs rampant within our society and needs to be carefully examined in your own life. Co-dependency is a false sense of affirmation and approval.

How am I co-dependent and with whom?

1) _____

2) _____

3) _____

4) _____

5) _____

OBSESSING

Obsessing can develop in any situation. It can be obsessing about a mate, money, controlling someone, or the future. I believe that obsessing is self-destructive. Obsessing over something isn't going to change things. It only will keep you upset, tense, and unsatisfied.

Decisions need to be made after honest deliberation of a situation, not only looking at how it will affect you, but also how it will affect others. Obsessive actions often led me to decisions I may not have made if I had taken the time to look at it. We cannot control other's feelings or thoughts or the future. It just can't be done. So, it is time to give up any idea of it.

Obsessing over something is not going to help anyone, and it will put a lot of stress in your life. There comes a time when we have to let go and let life take its course. Often times, people think that by obsessing over something that it is going to change the situation. It will not. This is an illusion. You are only damaging yourself. Get a hold of your mind. Make out that list of what is troubling you as mentioned previously and then make an action list. That is the best step you can take towards resolution.

What do I obsess over?

1) _____

2) _____

3) _____

4) _____

5) _____

NEEDS AND WANTS

I DO NOT NEED my husband! Yes, you heard that right. I DO NOT NEED him! I can take care of myself and provide for all of my own needs. I WANT my husband. That makes the difference between healthy and unhealthy behaviors and boundaries. I used to be co-dependent and NEEDED a man. That is no longer true since I worked through those issues. When someone asks you what you need or want, what is your reply: A million dollars, a new car, a nice home, love, acceptance? We all would like those things; however, it goes even deeper than material things. Needs and wants were something that, in my self-development process, I had to get clear on. For me, needs are things that keep you alive and functioning such as food, water, shelter, and health. Wants are the "nice to have."

When we get into a "have to have something badly" mode or "can't do without," we are now in addiction. This may be hard to hear but individuals must be careful of even having to have or NEEDING to have a child. A child may be wanted and desired. It is okay to have a passion to be a parent but when you get into an overly needy feeling, you may be operating out of dysfunction. If for some reason it works out that you cannot become a parent, it doesn't have to define you or your happiness. Would you be sad that it didn't work out? Of course! But we have to move forward and obtain other avenues of happiness. Our NEEDS come from God, our wants come from ourselves!

Now I do realize that a relationship is not needed to stay alive; however, if a person were the last survivor on earth, they would probably die much more quickly alone than if they had a companion. I agree that companionship is important, but I want you to hear the difference between companionship and co-dependency. The difference is having a healthy want instead of an unhealthy need for others. There are reports proving this with elderly or sick individuals who have a pet. They are much quicker to recover than someone alone. Companionship and affection are very important to our well-being. I classify this as a want and somewhat of a need, as long as the relationship is a healthy one and not a relationship out of addiction or co-dependency.

Wants are the things you desire or long for in your life ... like happiness, love, serenity, understanding, a good job, and of course, that new car. It is perfectly normal to want nice things, and not all of them have to be material goods. You deserve to have your wants met. Unfortunately, a person may get stuck in the notion that, because they want things, they are greedy. Maybe a parent said you were worthless and didn't deserve what you wanted, including love.

I remember as a young adult squabbling over something I wanted and my brother told me I shouldn't be so greedy and that there were children in Africa starving. My feelings were taken away and I felt like I was undeserving. I wondered how the children in Africa related to my wants. I also felt like somehow the children starving was partly my fault. If I weren't so selfish, then maybe they would not be starving. A child can't reason with statements such as this. Sometimes, people do get carried away with their wants, especially children because, well, they are children. As adults we have to keep a perspective on our wants and make sure it is not at the expense of someone else. However, putting the weight of the world on someone, especially a child, is not the answer.

When entering a relationship, we need to let others know our needs and wants in that particular relationship. This allows the other person to decide if he or she can provide those things. It is not fair to manipulate someone into doing something you want or need when it is against their desires. This can be difficult for a person from a dysfunctional family. Manipulation and control are the ways most of us were taught to get what we needed or wanted.

I'm sure you've heard or participated in conversations like, "Are you thirsty? I sure am." And then the person just sits there and sighs, making more comments about how thirsty they are. Finally the other person, tired of listening to them, unknowingly being manipulated, will eventually reply, "I'll get something for us to drink." This is the power of suggestion. It is a way to manipulate others into doing something you don't want to. The individual doesn't realize that they were just manipulated. Instead, a person might ask, "Will you please get me a drink?" This is straight forward and honest with your needs or wants.

If you are feeling the need for love and attention, then ask a person to take thirty minutes, or however long, and spend the time with you. This lets the person know exactly what you are wanting from them. And you will probably feel better about yourself that you were honest and didn't have to be manipulative. Now you are setting healthy boundaries and allowing the other person to have their boundaries.

You may begin practicing with small requests until you get enough confidence to express your deeper emotions about your wants and needs. An individual now has the opportunity to respond to your request. An important thing to remember is that the person you communicate with has every right to say "yes" or even "no" to your request. Do not take it personally. You want the same courtesy remember. Their reply may have nothing to do with you. We need to celebrate others for taking care of their own needs, wants, and setting boundaries.

What are things I have an unhealthy need for?

1) _____

2) _____

3) _____

4) _____

5) _____

GUILT, SHAME AND SHOULDS

One of the major contributors to making someone feel guilty or shameful are "shoulds." When you tell someone what they should be doing all of the time and that person does not have strong boundaries, then they will take on guilt or shame and eventually succumb to a person's wishes. When we say "yes" and we really want to say "no," it lowers our self-esteem because we did not stand up for ourselves. So then we have guilt, shame and lower self-esteem that all feed on one another, keeping us down for the count. The key is to remember that we have a choice, and there are no excuses.

When someone starts telling you what you should do, politely tell them you appreciate their advice; however, you will be the only person determining what works for you, and what doesn't. This quickly takes the power away from them and places it back in your hands where it belongs. Let's take a look at other statements that reflect guilt being used to manipulate.

- We sacrificed all of these years raising you, feeding and clothing you, and look at what we get in return
- Your father may not live much longer, so don't you think you can give up this nonsense
- You should help us out, we were always there with food in your mouth and clothes on your back
- That's okay, don't worry about me, I'll be all right, even though I'm really not doing well…you go on about your business
- You are ungrateful after all that we have done for you
- If you really loved me, you would find it in your heart to do this one thing I've asked of you
- You are selfish and do not think of anyone except yourself
- I gave birth to you, you should do this for me, you owe me

I call these statements "sideways guilt," because the individual does not come right out and put guilt on someone. It is done in a sneaky, manipulative way so that you don't even know what hit you until you have already succumbed to their behavior. And truly, the feeling usually runs deeper than normal guilt and slides into shame. Through the practice of setting boundaries and writing about the dysfunction, you can learn what to listen and watch out for. People usually use the same types of statements when projecting guilt.

What guilt statements do I replay in my head?

1) _____

2) _____

3) _____

4) _____

5) _____

Now reframe these statements into positive statements to let them go:

1) _____

2) _____

3) _____

4) _____

5) _____

SADNESS

Throughout my work in self-development, I've seen myself and others go through a lot of sadness. I believe this has to do with the grieving process we experience about our childhood and the sense of loss we feel. Sadness may come and go as we grieve different parts of our life and experiences. Sadness also tends to cycle in with other feelings. When my mother died, I felt sadness, anger, and joy. One feeling will usually transition into another feeling.

You must experience all of your feelings to complete a cycle of emotions. It doesn't mean the feelings will be gone forever. It just means the initial overwhelming feelings will lessen over time. It is natural that ten years from now I will still have sadness that my mother is gone or that my upbringing wasn't perfect. However, you don't want to stay stuck in those feelings either. It is not an excuse not to perform. The important thing is, and this is true of all feelings, that you express and experience them. This is essential to your well-being. If you suppress feelings, they will only build up over time until they all come rushing to the surface at once with overwhelming results, emotionally and physically. Suppressed feelings are only going to fester in the body and, over time, cause illness.

What do I still hang onto sadness for?

Example: my mother not showing me love

1) _____

2) _____

3) _____

4) _____

5) _____

ANGER

For me, anger is probably one of the hardest emotions to experience. It is especially hard letting others see me angry. I was told that you should not get angry, yell or scream. Now I know this is nonsense. I'm here to tell you it is probably the healthiest thing you can do, if that is the emotion you are experiencing. All feelings have a right to be experienced and this doesn't exclude anger.

Being that we came from dysfunctional families, we may have experienced a lot of anger from others, possibly through physical and verbal abuse. However, feeling and expressing your anger does not give you a license to abuse others or to be explosive or inappropriate with the feeling. Abuse is blaming others. Being dysfunctional is about being immature. It is time to grow up and take responsibility and express yourself to benefit your well-being.

I had a hard time experiencing my anger because I believed that if I did, then the people seeing me would leave. This is fear of abandonment. I remember my father getting angry and I would feel very threatened. One time, when my father was home from traveling on the road, he had too much to drink. My father had a love for knives and even named his favorite one "Maude." He was showing "Maude" and several others off by throwing them into our bedroom door. My mother got angry and proceeded to do nothing but herd us behind her, and we all three watched him be proud of himself and his knives. I remember being very afraid of him drinking and experiencing these kind of events. There was always an undertone of anger about him.

My mother obviously felt threatened to show her anger and my father usually showed his in an uncaring, almost vengeful way. You could feel it in the air. I believe my father and mother boiled with anger most of the time, being stuck in it and unable to move into little else. A lot of the time, what I have noticed happens with anger is that people don't have boundaries. Here is an example:

Let's say a friend gets angry and I don't know why. I start to feel uncomfortable with her anger and start to take it on as my own. Or maybe I am so uncomfortable with anger that my fear comes up, and then I start to tell my friend not to be angry and comfort her.

In both of these situations, I would not be setting a boundary with my friend's anger. Who said it had anything to do with me? It is important to have boundaries with others and their emotions. It is important to show children boundaries with other individual's emotions by setting boundaries yourself.

Anger can be expressed in a lot of constructive ways, such as yelling into a pillow or striking a pillow with your fists. You do not have to fear anger. However, releasing anger is not appropriate when you are inflicting pain on someone else or yourself. If you feel like you have a true anger problem, I would recommend seeking a professional to assist you.

What ways do I show inappropriate anger?

1) _____

2) _____

3) _____

4) _____

5) _____

RESENTMENT

If you constantly radiate resentment, what do you think will come back to you? Resentment is the part of anger that is boiling, seething and destructive. If you are constantly boiling, there is no space for peace. No space for closure. Resentment can eat at you until it takes a toll physically, emotionally, mentally, and spiritually.

It is understandable, coming from a family of dysfunction, that an individual may have some unresolved feelings. I don't feel like anyone has to forget their experiences. There comes a time, though, when we must let go to start living our life. You will not gain anything from holding on to resentment. There is no time like the present to start living and let go of those things that hold you back. It is time to look at forgiveness. Who do you need to forgive? Why can you not forgive? What belief holds you back? What feeling holds you back? Tell me, what would life look like if you didn't live with the resentment? What could you do with that time and energy?

RESENTMENT EXERCISE:

Take a look at all of the areas in your life where you may be holding on to resentment. It is time to let it go. You may not realize just how much it is affecting your life and your body. Here is an example of a great way to work through resentment. You can also use this with emotions such as anger, fear, and sadness, or behaviors such as control and manipulation.

EXAMPLE:

I resent my father.

Cause: He chose to give me up and not spend time with me. He visited rarely, even though he would pass through town often when he was an entertainer.

Effects:

Self-esteem: I feel like I've been "bad" and undeserving of his attention.

Worth: I feel unworthy of his attention. I feel like I didn't do something right. I feel unimportant when he does not want to see me.

Fear: I fear I'm not worthy of having a lasting relationship. Everyone will eventually leave.

These are the messages that we get:

1) I am a bad person
2) I am undeserving
3) I am not worthy
4) My needs do not come first
5) I will always be abandoned
6) I have to "do" more to win his love

EXAMPLE USING CONTROL:

I feel a need to control my husband.

Cause: My family members were always abandoning me physically and emotionally. I tried my best through my behavior to keep them around and please them, but it seemed to get worse.

Effects:

Worth: I felt unworthy of having loving people around me who will not leave me.

Fear: I fear that if I don't control what is going on around me that everything will fall apart.

Terrified: I feel terrified that my spouse will leave me just like everyone else, and so I have to do everything can to prevent it from happening.

These are the messages that we get:

1) I am not worthy
2) I do not deserve an honest relationship
3) Individuals will always abandon me
4) I have to live in terror

Use this exercise for all of the relationships in your life. Be honest with yourself. After each exercise, re-read the NEW positive beliefs you created for yourself to turn around the negative belief. Remember to read these each day to change your thought process.

PROJECTING

There are two types of projecting that I want to explain to you. The first is projecting your feelings onto someone else, and the second is projecting problems into the future. Let's take a look at the difference.

PROJECTING FEELINGS ONTO OTHERS:

You're probably wondering how you can project feelings onto someone else. In actuality, it probably happens quite a bit without your being aware of it. For instance, have you ever been with someone that you really wanted to talk about an issue with. Maybe you were having some feelings that were difficult to hold back; however, you hesitated discussing them. You hint around by asking, "Is everything okay?", "Are you sure you don't want to talk about something?" Instead of just opening up and talking about how you feel, you try and project your feelings of discomfort so that the other individual will open a discussion, and then you can blame it on them for starting it. Sound familiar? This is projection and manipulation. Remember, power of suggestion.

Any feelings can be projected, including anger, fear, or even judgment. A dear friend of mine would call me to talk about her relationship with her boyfriend. She only told me about the pain she was experiencing and the stress she experienced in the relationship. She asked me what she should do. I explained that I did not hear or see her experiencing happiness and that maybe she could evaluate taking a break from the relationship so that it would allow her to assess her situation and her feelings. She agreed that I might be right; however, she stayed in the relationship for some time. I had to resign myself from giving advice or opinions on the relationship even though she asked me for it. She came to me at a later time after she broke off the abusive relationship and then accused me of being judgmental and unsupportive during her relationship with this man. I couldn't win.

I was upset that she felt I was judgmental and unsupportive because that was not true to my feelings. I heard her continual pain. When she asked for advice, what I had to tell her would have helped get her out of the destructive relationship. She didn't want to hear that, even though it is what happened in the end. With her continual confrontation and projecting judgment on me, I had to set a boundary of distance with her until she stopped projecting and blaming me for what actually had nothing to do with me.

Sometimes it is hard to face the truth, and we turn around and blame someone we have asked for guidance. We project feelings of judgment, jealousy, fear, anger, and so on. Keeping separate states of being is important to keeping separate feelings.

PROJECTING PROBLEMS INTO THE FUTURE:

We all want to make plans for the future. However, do you want to make plans for pain and problems for the future? Sounds ridiculous, right? Constant worrying about "what could happen" is doing just that. You set yourself up for all types of scenarios about all of the horrible things that might happen and how you would handle them.

What happened to today? We can't live today fully while constantly projecting the future and its possible bumps in the road. You could go a whole lifetime worrying and miss out on the opportunity to enjoy today. Stop and ask yourself, "What would you like to do today?" Projecting problems keeps us in our past behaviors and does not allow us to enjoy the present. When we are projecting problems, we are staying in the behavior of being a victim and letting the fear control our lives. No one knows exactly what will happen in the future. We can only make plans and adjust accordingly to life as it happens. You will be much happier staying with today.

How do I project my feelings?

1) _____

2) _____

3) _____

4) _____

5) _____

GETTING REAL

Occasionally, we all say one thing and think another. Why do we keep to ourselves how we really feel about things? Possibly, the answer is people pleasing, approval seeking, or fear of showing yourself to others. When you are not being real and true to whom you are and your feelings, happiness is going to be difficult to achieve. Can you be happy knowing people love a facade? Are you fearful that if they see the real you they will no longer love you? If that is the case, then I would say you are better off without them.

If no one in the universe loved you, how would you feel? Can you accept only self love and approval? The feelings involved with this question alone can motivate us towards self-development and awareness. If you are pretending you are someone you are not and receiving acceptance and strokes through it, your self-esteem deep within will be low, knowing you are not being real. Strokes alone will not satisfy the inner soul.

My father always talked badly about my brother in front of me. My father and brother did not speak the last twenty years of my father's life. Dad was always telling me what a cowardly, weak, unsuccessful, untalented person my brother was. Interestingly, later I found out that my father only had good things to say about my brother when he was talking about him in front of his step-children, whom he lived with and spent much time around. My father was so fearful of not being top dog. He was afraid of my brother, and even worse, my sister or me, being women and having more success than he had. He, like my mother, played us all against each other and told enormous lies to do so. Family secrets were habitual.

As children growing up in dysfunction, we developed skills of projecting different faces such as happiness to survive. This kept our world, as we knew it, from shattering. However, it doesn't work in the long run. We can't pretend and really enjoy our lives and who we are. Our subconscious knows the truth, whether we are consciously aware or not. To stop pretending and get real, you have to let go of trying to get acceptance from others.

You have to take a non-caring attitude, and, what I mean by that is that you won't let anybody stand in the way of you being yourself.

It is not your problem if they don't like the real, honest you. I can tell you from experience that when I've taken an honest approach, I usually receive more love from a person than when I was trying to be someone else. People like honesty. They may not like you; however, they will respect you for being real.

When starting a self-development program, I honestly believe that if you are single, stay that way for at least a year. Take a year off from any romantic relationships. I know this may sound impossible. It is not. This gives you time to establish a solid foundation for your self-development program. During this time you can work on developing your wants, needs, and setting boundaries. After the year off, then you can move slowly into dating and relationships. My self-esteem and self-worth really grew when I took the time to concentrate on my own needs. This was the way I could keep myself real.

MINIMIZING

When we deny how bad things were when we were children or what we are currently experiencing, we are minimizing circumstances. Maybe those beatings weren't really so bad, or mom really told us those bad things about ourselves because she wanted us to be strong adults. Or, our marriage isn't really that bad. Individuals try minimizing things, hoping eventually they will just go away. However, things don't just go away.

By minimizing your experiences, you are taking your own state of being away. The messages you received are that you really don't know what you are talking about. How can you trust yourself? We are each entitled to experience the full impact an event had on us so we can evaluate exactly what happened. You may not understand what happened; however, you do not have to minimize it either. We cannot work through the pain by minimizing conditions. Take a deep breath, relax, and let the memories come to you as they happen.

What things are you minimizing?

1) _____

Why? _____

2) _____

Why? _____

3) _____

Why? _____

4) _____

Why? _____

5) _____

Why? _____

THE VICTIM

In the dysfunction I grew up in, I was raised to portray a victim. I was taught to react instead of act, which gave others power over me. As I grew up, I had a craving to fulfill a sick need for a relationship that resembled my dysfunctional childhood setting. Pain took the place of love. Pity from others meant attention and eventually a feeling of being loved, even though it was misguided.

Adult children of dysfunction were victims as children. No one can take away the fact that you were mistreated as a child. However, to remain a victim is to remain weak. Eventually people who pity you will think you are pathetic. Somewhere in your mind, you may even realize you are being pathetic. No one enjoys the company of someone who stands defenseless all of the time. More than likely, the individuals around a victim will end up leaving, and then the victim has once again reinforced their feelings of being worthless.

We cannot get out of the dysfunctional behavior if we do not stop being a victim. It takes a decision to just do it. I wish there was some magic dust we could just sprinkle on ourselves, and "poof," the behavior is gone. It takes work and dedication to go through our past in order to develop our future. You are a strong person and you have what it takes.

How are you playing the victim?

1) _____

Why? _____

2) _____

Why? _____

3) _____

Why? _____

4) _____

Why? _____

5) _____

Why? _____

LOYALTY

What is it that holds us loyal to individuals who continually abuse us and let us down? It is fear, plain and simple, yet, complex in nature. In all families, whether healthy or dysfunctional, there is usually a code of ethics within the family and the role we play with each person. We are taught that blood kin have an unbreakable connection, and therefore, we should remain loyal. First of all, any message with a "should" in it needs to be examined carefully. The only thing I feel like you should do is to take care of your own needs and wants and listen to what your body is telling you. This brings me to talking about being loyal to yourself. Please understand, not all "shoulds" are bad. We have to discern them.

If you are not being loyal to yourself, you cannot be loyal to others. It just doesn't work. Eventually, the pain will catch up with you. We can spend a lot of energy feeling guilty and ashamed if we are not loyal to our parents. The fact is that your parent/caregiver chose to have and keep you, but that does not give them grounds to call in favors or loyalty. If being loyal to someone means giving up a part of yourself, then I feel the individual is not being loyal to you, your needs and wants and neither are you. Go within yourself to find the answer. Ask yourself, "Am I honoring myself?" If you find the answer is anything except a definite "yes," then it is time to start honoring who you are and your wants and needs.

How am I being loyal to dysfunctional situations?

1) _____

Why? _____

How does it hold me back?

_____

2) _____

Why? _____

How does it hold me back?

_____

3) _____

Why? _____

How does it hold me back?

_____

4) _____

Why? _____

How does it hold me back?

_____

5) _____

Why? _____

How does it hold me back?

_____

PARALYSIS

Can you imagine being afraid of fun or enjoyment? How about social activities, going to work, or even simple tasks such as shopping and driving? Growing up in an abusive home, many individuals I have known, including myself, have found activities such as these difficult to perform. If an individual has experienced abuse at the hands of their own family, it is not surprising that they would grow up with enormous amount of fear about the rest of the world.

Victims of abuse have more than likely grown up without trust in people, which paralyzes them in relationships. If someone, such as a parent, told them they loved them and then abused them, what would make a person think they could trust anyone else? So, to avoid getting involved in relationships of any type, an individual, probably knowingly or unknowingly, protects themselves by not getting involved in social activities or any type of functions.

A lot of seriousness is involved in growing up in an abusive home. It is hard to laugh and play when you are constantly on guard. I tended to build a protective shield around my body and emotions, preventing others from reaching inside, which also means fun and laughter often got squelched. Without learning how to relax and enjoy fun and laughter as an adult, it becomes easy to get paralyzed in an environment of such activities because it is something we were not allowed to experience as children. If we started to relax and enjoy ourselves, and a parent would come along to scold us for doing so; these messages told us it was not safe to have fun.

When my husband left me the first time, and then I accepted him back, I became paralyzed within my home. I would rush home after work to make sure he had not left me again. I was constantly monitoring the home and phone calls, reassuring myself he had not left. I was afraid to venture out of my own home because of this paralyzing fear. If I was at home then he couldn't pack up. Before this incident happened, I had already learning paralyzing behavior from my mother by her not having any friends or social activities.

You can also get caught up in paralyzing behavior at work. If you are experiencing a lot of chaos in your personal life, it can prevent you from thinking about anything else except the problem. We cannot live healthy, productive lives like this. It is time to take your power back from the chaos and use it in your healing process. Let's take a look at some of the ways you might be paralyzed and then at some of the ways to take action.

PARALYZING BEHAVIORS:

- Not having any friends
- Not being involved in social activities or functions
- Watching too many hours of television
- Not leaving the house except for work or errands
- Not accepting dates or invitations
- Worrying about issues uncontrollably
- Inability to concentrate
- Not communicating your feelings, thoughts and ideas
- Procrastinating

POSITIVE ACTIONS TOWARDS CHANGE:

- Developing friendships by getting involved in an activity such as a pottery class, cooking class, motivational seminar, or anything you find fun and interesting
- Instead of sitting in front of the TV, go outside and take a walk or a bike ride
- Accept a date to go out to a casual dinner and a movie or call someone and invite them out
- Join a group that will help you learn how to speak and communicate your ideas and opinions
- Take a class at a local community college, you will learn something new and meet new people
- Volunteer your services to a local charity
- Take a weekend trip to a bed and breakfast
- Test drive a new car you've been keeping your eye on
- Go to a self-help group meeting

How do I act out being paralyzed?

1) _____

2) _____

3) _____

4) _____

5) _____

ACCOUNTABLE

Working on your issues and being honest with yourself also means being accountable for your actions. It's time to grow up! As disappointing as that may be, we must accept adulthood and responsibility for what happens presently in our lives. This doesn't mean we have to be accountable for what happened to us as children. We were dependent on someone else for most everything. We were not responsible. Our parents are accountable for how they raised us. This doesn't give us the green light; however, to blame our parents for everything that is not right in our lives in the present. If an individual has become conscious of his or her dysfunction, there are no excuses. It is time to take a look within.

We need to make peace with ourselves and, to do so; we need to be accountable for our lives. You cannot have peace while constantly making someone else accountable for how your life is going. Within ourselves, we have all of the answers we need. Now is the time to trust and listen to yourself for these answers.

What do I need to be accountable for?

1) _____

2) _____

3) _____

4) _____

5) _____

BLAME

Continually blaming others for our problems takes a lot of energy. Why not use that energy to get the life you dream about. Blaming will never get you what you really want. Blaming becomes easy for people because then they feel like they do not have to live up to any-one's expectations. If your parents blamed you consistently, you could never meet their expectations. Children of dysfunctional families tend to turn the blame around on their parents to ease their feelings of low self-esteem during adulthood.

Be accountable for your own actions, and if you are wrong, prompt-ly admit it. Admitting it even just to yourself can release you from the behavior of blaming others. We do not have to forget what happened to us as children. Our caregivers may never change. We can only work on our own life and live for our present moment. We can make our parents accountable in our self-development work for what they did, and release that negative energy.

Who am I still blaming?

1) _____

2) _____

3) _____

4) _____

5) _____

FORGIVING

Whoever said, "forgive and forget?" I don't think was an individual who was experiencing their emotions. It is perfectly okay to forgive; however, to forget, you may be in denial of a situation you had to give forgiveness to in the first place. Remembering what has happened to us keeps us out of denial and helps us to maintain boundaries to prevent similar situations from recurring. Remembering doesn't mean that we have to stay in the pain.

When we remember past unpleasant events, we can feel inspired by the new person we have created in ourselves by being conscious, brave, and making changes. It isn't easy going through all of the change and then all of the sudden forget what motivated us to change in the first place.

Forgiving takes a lot of work and time, and each person must decide for themselves what the best way is for them to do that. Throughout my self-development process, I have met individuals who felt like they did not want to forgive others. Some individuals feel like it is absolutely necessary to forgive.

I don't believe I have to only feel one way. It is a wonderful concept thinking that you can forgive once and for all. However, I know that in life there are certain circumstances that arise and tip off those old feelings toward your offender. It isn't very easy to say, "Oh yeah, I already forgave this person, silly me, I can't feel this way anymore." This is a "should" and it doesn't belong in our lives.

The truth is that we may have unforgiving feelings come up after initially forgiving someone. When they do, we just have to recognize them, feel them, and work through them to be able to release them. Ask God to help you once again forgive. And ask for God to forgive you.

Sometimes I can forgive my parents for their actions, and sometimes I cannot. I don't hold on to the feelings. I just experience them while I am having them, and that helps me let go. Then I pray to God to help me!

Who do I need to forgive?

1) _____

What holds me back?

_____

2) _____

What holds me back?

_____

3) _____

What holds me back?

_____

4) _____

What holds me back?

_____

5) _____

What holds me back?

_____

TRUST

When I used to hear the word "trust," I would sort of chuckle, thinking to myself, "right," like I'm going to trust anything or anyone. To me, trust was for idiots who didn't want to hear the truth. My mother always gave us the message, "Men will always lie, cheat, and leave you." My father consistently proved her right. I trusted my mother was right from what I saw and heard. She appeared to be a very wise woman. I wanted to be strong like her. I woke up and got conscious when that wish started to become a reality. I realized she wasn't that strong after all. However, if I didn't trust what my mother had told me, then I would be saying she was wrong all of her life. That is when I had to let go of her belief system and make my own, as we discussed previously in Chapter One.

There are some individuals who trust too much, believing everything and everyone. The tabloids thank God for these people. Trust is something you need to build with another person. If trust is given too quickly, you may get hurt easily. However, this is not cause to not trust at all. Just take your time and build a relationship before jumping in blindly with someone you really don't know.

When trust has been broken, it is hard to regain it with the individual that you feel betrayed by. It becomes hard to trust new individuals. It is hard not to judge someone and decide your trust level with them based on past experiences. Taking the past into consideration, you can find a trust level with which you are comfortable and go from there. You have the right to never trust someone who has caused you pain or harm in a highly destructive way. However, that's not to say that you can hang on to mistrust if you CHOOSE to remain in the relationship. That is not fair to that person.

Usually, children trust people more easily because they are led to believe adults would not betray them. This is why a lot adults prey on children. When we lose our trust at an early age, it can become part of our belief system not to trust.

My father hardly ever paid child support. One time when I was about fourteen, he told me he would send me some money, as if he were doing me a favor. It was a particularly difficult time financially for my mother, and I was already working part time. My mother did not finish high school and found it difficult to find a decent paying job.

My father sent me a series of checks within a short period of time, each for sixty dollars. I had cashed them at a drug store that my mother and I frequently shopped. They knew us well and allowed us to cash checks. A couple of weeks later, the store manager informed my mother and I that all three checks had bounced and they had tried running the checks through the bank several times without success.

Dad swore he didn't know why they bounced and that there was money in his account. I felt humiliated and ashamed. At this point, my trust in my father was already gone, and this was a major factor in my continual feelings of distrust for others.

To have healthy relationships, we must be respectful of others if we hope to gain and keep their trust. Trust is a two way street!

Who am I still not trusting?

1) _____

Why? _____

How does it hold me back?

_____

2) _____

Why? _____

How does it hold me back?

_____

3) _____

Why? _____

How does it hold me back?

_____

4) _____

Why? _____

How does it hold me back?

_____

5) _____

Why? _____

How does it hold me back?

_____

JUDGMENT

In dysfunctional families a lot of judgment is usually placed on others. Most judgment is improperly used. Dysfunctional parents will sometimes use particular circumstances unjustly to place blame and judgment on a child. For example, if a father is molesting his daughter, the mother may lay blame on the daughter, and pronounce judgment such as, "You are a dirty and bad girl." This allows the mother to blame the daughter instead of admitting her husband could betray her.

When growing up in a dysfunctional family, it is easy to have lost the ability to trust others. When we go out into life, scrutiny often comes in to play. I have seen many friends who quickly judge a person when they initially meet them. The judgment usually comes through the voice, a look in the eye, or their body language. It becomes hard to develop friends when executing this behavior.

I do believe we need to take caution when interacting with others and listen to our intuition; however, a healthy balance of politeness and awareness is essential. "Do unto others as you would have them do unto you." This is a good life rule. Remember how you feel when you are being judged? It doesn't feel nice, and we may also be missing out on an opportunity for a good friendship. New positive beliefs are a great way to replace those old negative beliefs you once heard, which I feel are nothing but judgments.

How am I judgmental?

1) _____

2) _____

3) _____

4) _____

5) _____

INVENTORIES

An important part of understanding where you are is figuring out where you have been. Completing an inventory is a great way of doing just that! It helps you to figure out many of your patterns, healthy or not, as well as the people in your life. It will help you in being able to determine needed changes or discover why things happened a certain way. You can complete an inventory by telling stories or making lists of individuals or situations. Let's take a look:

"PAST" INVENTORY EXAMPLE:

When I was about nine, I had saved up enough money to buy my mother a birthday present that she had admired. It had a geode bottom and out of the center came a piece of wire shaped into a heart. At the top center of the heart was a small dangling amethyst. It was $15.00. I remember feeling so proud of buying it and that my mother would be so happy. When I gave it to her, much to my surprise, she seemed disappointed.

We were broke at the time and my mother was struggling to survive and provide for both me and my older sister. She explained to me how we needed the money and that she was going to return it for the cash. I felt very hurt. I was also scared about our financial dilemma. We both went to the store where I bought it and she started to return it. She and the store employees could sense my pain and my mother decided not to return it; however, it didn't make my pain go away. I still think about that gift with sadness and the shame I felt. I wanted her to accept my gift of love.

"PRESENT" INVENTORY EXAMPLE:

I notice myself being controlling with my husband as far as money and bills are concerned. I feel scared that he won't be responsible and that we may lose everything. He says he is trying. I am also angry that he won't be more responsible. When I am angry, I feel unsafe and vulnerable.

Notice in both the past and present journal, that she wrote about her feelings surrounding the events in her life. Remember, it is okay to get assistance from someone you feel safe with if you are having difficulty while journaling. When you first start journaling, you may only be writing about your experiences, whether past or present. When you have been journaling for some time, you will find that while writing, your feelings will start to become present for you to deal with. Often times, feelings are repressed and this is a way to open them up. Give yourself plenty of opportunity and understanding. As you finish journaling, say a NEW positive belief to yourself to affirm you are okay.

RELATIONSHIP INVENTORIES:

The great thing about working on inventories is that they can be applied to any aspect of your life. A great way to determine how you interact in relationships is to inventory the behavior. You can utilize inventories with relationships, behaviors, feelings, even how you interact with money. Below we will look at an example of a relationship inventory. Just begin by listing the names of the individuals you have been involved with and then write about how you interacted with them. Then, write a second perspective on how these individuals interacted with you. What similarities did you find? What kind of person have you been attracting? To further the inventory, write about how your parents' behaviors were similar.

EXAMPLE:

June is going to write about the men she has dated. (On this inventory, she will evaluate her behaviors in the relationships).

BOB:

CONTROLLING:
I would tell him that if he didn't do things the way I wanted to that I could find someone who would.

MANIPULATIVE:

Bob wanted to spend the evening with his buddies without me. I made myself start crying and I called him right before he was to leave. I told him that I was really upset and I really needed him to come and stay the night with me. When he said he already had plans, I started crying more, telling him that obviously I wasn't worth it for him to come be with me. He ended up coming over and canceled his plans.

SHAME:

I would always tell him that he shouldn't feel a particular way, that it was wrong and ask him how he could be the way he was.

PEOPLE PLEASING:

I would buy him expensive gifts all of the time and give him cards so that he wouldn't get angry with me and leave.

CONTROLLING WITH SEX:

I would tell Bob that if he was "good" or bought me a present that maybe I would let him stay the night.

GUILT:

I would tell Bob that other men in the past spent more time and energy on me and that he should do more to keep me happy.

After June did the inventory on "Bob," she would list out each person she has had a romantic relationship with so that she can draw correlations among those she is attracting. This is what you will do. I did many different kinds of inventories. I think the important thing was for me to be journaling all of the time on my past and present experiences so I could connect the dots and make my future a better one!

LETTING GO

You've probably heard the term, "Let go, Let God." Before self-development work when I heard this statement, my response was something more like, "Get a grip!" It sounds like that came straight out of my controlling issues. Isn't it ironic that when someone is telling me to let go, I would tell them to "Get a grip?" Letting go isn't as simple as it is made to sound. You have to consider all of the years you've dealt with unhappiness or pain. I wish it were as easy as one day throwing away all the negative stuff. But in a sense, that is exactly what you have to do.

Letting go of issues doesn't mean having to forget. It means deciding that in order to get on and lead a happy life, you need to let go of old behaviors and thought processes. There comes a time in life when you have to do this or it will slow you down. Because trust was so difficult in our family of origin, it is hard to let go of the issues and trust that someone else (such as God) will take care our problem.

When I first started working my own self-development program, I would read about turning my problems over to my higher power and that they would be "taken care of." How was I going to turn over my issues when I couldn't feel the presence of God? Just saying the word "God" made me twitch uncomfortably inside. However, it worked. With time and working on my journal, I was able to start to feel my emotions. More and more, I found myself trusting the self-development work and letting things go. In time I began to trust in God and turn things over.

Remember, not being able to let go is a trust and manipulation issue. Once we begin working on these two things, letting go becomes easier.

Some of my personal thoughts and perceived opinions on what causes much of the dysfunction follow:

VERBAL ABUSE

Verbal abuse is possibly the hardest to define and recognize. The bruises from verbal abuse affect all five of the states of being: mental, emotional, physical, spiritual, and sexual. My experience has shown me that it can be difficult to prove or even recognize. I would say that most of us were brought up to believe our parents are always right and that they know best. Why wouldn't we believe this? They love us, right? However, does someone that loves you put you down, discredit you, and tell you that you are worthless? Maybe we are told, "It's for your best," or "If you weren't so bad, I wouldn't have to say these things."

Verbal abuse for me is when someone continually and hurtfully puts me down so that they may gain power over me. It felt like my parents or peers started verbally abusing me so that they would have control over my life. My experience has been that if you were brought up in a dysfunctional family, it is likely your parents grew up in a dysfunctional family. I don't think verbal abuse is usually something that someone all of the sudden decides to start doing. I feel verbal abuse comes out of bottled anger and the fear of not being in control.

There were small things continually said to me as a child that I felt uncomfortable with; however, they were passed off as "normal ridicule." I remember my family always teasing me about not being able to tie my shoes. Up until my family's deaths, I still heard, "Been tying your shoes long?" It was a joke going back to when I was trying to learn how to tie my shoes, and I was to hear about it for a long time after. Apparently, I had trouble learning because I was being shown two different ways to tie my shoes, and I was getting confused with my parents arguing about who had the right way. This goes deeper as to feelings of not wanting to let either parent down or show preference.

We have to remember that as adults, what we think is a joke to us may seriously affect a child's self-esteem if the joke persists. This continual joke accelerated my feelings of being stupid and shameful. In extreme verbal abuse cases, these individuals will probably grow up to be approval seeking persons, always looking for validation outside of themselves.

If someone continually tells you that you are worthless, it is hard not to take on what they are saying as a belief. The belief is even stronger when someone you trust is the one telling you these negative things. So why would a parent or adult verbally abuse a child or person? Before, I explained that the person may try to maintain control over an individual. I have noticed in personal experiences that the abuser has experienced dysfunctional situations first hand. As a child from a dysfunctional family, they may learn how to control and abuse others at an early age. You can start to track these childhood issues and behaviors through journaling and writing inventories. Through these activities you can learn the role you and your parents played in the dysfunction.

EXAMPLE:

Daughter writing about her mother:

My mother always said I was worthless and good for nothing, that no man would have me, and that I shouldn't even try because I'm ugly and don't deserve a nice man. She told me that she's the only one that could love me because she was my mother and she was supposed to.

Intent of mother whether conscious or unconscious:

To reverse roles with the child and set her up as a caregiver so that the child never abandons her mother. The child will feel responsible for her mother's needs before her own interests and needs. Setting this up, the mother does not feel threatened. The child's self-esteem is low and they feel a responsibility towards the mother for loving her when no one else would.

Parents tell me it is hard to let go of children as they grow up. For a dysfunctional family that does not have boundaries, the task seems even greater. It is normal for parents to have fear and sadness as their children no longer depend on them. If a child has been put in the role of the caregiver, taking care of their parents' emotions and needs, the parents lose a sense of security when their child ventures out of the web. The parents may feel if they ridicule their child enough, the child will not seek outside relationships and therefore depend more on the family. I do not feel like parents always do this consciously; however, that is also not an excuse. We all deserve to be treated with respect and kindness. Verbal abuse happens for many different reasons and it is important for you to break the cycle.

PHYSICAL ABUSE

Unlike verbal abuse, with physical abuse, you always know when you are being attacked. Likely, individuals do have the bruises and proof to show they were abused. Still, to this day, I am bewildered, even though I understand intellectually, what makes a person strike their child. Like verbal abuse, the offender may be trying to gain control over the one being abused.

I have heard reports that many of the abusers were abused themselves. You would think that out of their pain they would know how it feels and that they would not become abusers themselves. But, this is how powerful belief systems are and the reason why we need to examine them.

I believe individuals shut their emotions down to survive and then rage and anger surface. Most victims are dependent on the abuser for food and shelter. The victim may feel like there is no place to go and no one to safely tell without destroying everyone and everything familiar to them. We are dependent on our caregivers as infants for survival, so it seems natural that a child might think that if they go for help outside of their parents, and their parents are taken away, they might die. Who would take care of them? A child probably wouldn't be able to reason this. The fear has already been deeply instilled.

Abusers can inflict guilt on the victim to convince them that they are right in their actions. The abuser may say things like, "If you weren't so bad I wouldn't have to do this," or "This hurts me as much as it hurts you." This verbal abuse, along with physical abuse can instill a belief that the victim is worthless and a "bad" individual.

My mother's grandmother (my great, great grandmother) gave her a butcher knife beating on her legs when she was a little girl. My grandfather came into the room and stopped her. My mother told me that the other family members had to restrain my grandfather from killing my great grandmother.

My mother also told me that she was physically afraid of my father, even though he only tried hitting her once. She says he didn't hit her again after she hit him back. She was afraid on a larger scale. Twice that I can clearly remember, my mother hid me at friends' houses so that my father would not have access to me. She was fearful he might try and take me. It was a bizarre feeling hiding out from my father. I was still in a lot of denial about just how bad things were.

My brother told me stories of my father beating him. He would literally hit my brother in the stomach in front of his friends. He demanded that my brother "be a man," something that seemed to be lacking from my father.

My father had a large imagination that went along with his enormous lies. He would say things to make us believe he was part of the Mafia. My sister later met people in Chicago who seemed to think he really was. When I was about thirteen, he told me on the phone that he was going to put a "hit" out on my mother. All of my life I heard stories about how he was trying to "get out of the business" and therefore he was always on the run. He used many different aliases. He would use different disguised voices and names on his telephone answering machine. If he was making threats against my own mother, what would make me think he wouldn't do harm to me?

In phone conversations, my dad would accuse my mother of having slept around with other men. He would tell me how he had crippled a man by slitting his hamstrings because she was sleeping with him. My sister seemed to believe the story since my mother did not deny it and ultimately feared my father. He would say things to promote my thinking he was a hit man. Who can decipher the truth from all of that garbage? Dad was a sociopath. He had no conscience.

I had two different approaches and feelings towards my father: One was that I loathed him and didn't like him for not being what I wanted or needed. The second was that I was graced with knowing him as a talented musician and a person who, in an off-hand way, gave me experiences in my life that have helped make me a stronger person today. I could just condemn all of the bad experiences; however, light does comes out of the dark.

Many individuals get trapped in the fear of the possible loss of relations with their parents or peers who are abusive. These are choices we have to make. I do not suggest that anyone go through these situations alone. There are many resources for help.

SEXUAL ABUSE

Sexual abuse is a form of physical abuse that, unfortunately, doesn't always outwardly show bruises or proof of injustice. However, it has a lot of mental, emotional, physical, spiritual, and of course, sexual scarring. Sexual abuse can also include a great deal of verbal abuse. The perpetrator may use verbal abuse to scare a victim into not telling anyone of the abuse. Threats may be made such as "I will kill you if you tell", "I will not love you anymore", or "No one will believe you and then they will hate you."

A young child may not know why an adult wouldn't be telling the truth. Even with the abuse, we are usually given the understanding that parents are supposed to love their child. The abuse may become a substitute for love. Like other abusive situations, the victim may rely on the perpetrator for food and shelter, and may feel they do not have anyone they can go to for help.

There are numerous ways a victim may have been manipulated into the abuse and kept silent about it. In my experience, if these secrets remain silenced, they will never go away. I do believe it takes a brave, conscious, and strong person to break this chain. It isn't easy to confront or leave the only environment you have known, and as a child, it's almost impossible. However, if you do not confront these issues as an adult, you are likely going to pass it on to your children and continue to live an unhappy life.

When sexually abused, you are not given healthy messages about what is appropriate and what is inappropriate behavior. As an adult, it may become difficult to develop healthy and long lasting relationships and to be able to set healthy boundaries. Sexual difficulties and trust issues come up again and again unless you work them out.

There comes a time in a relationship, if you are about to become sexual with your spouse, you may need to discuss your sexual needs and boundaries. You do not always have to divulge your experience with sexual abuse. However, if you are expecting a long term relationship, I do feel it is pertinent to discuss your experience. Relationships are based on trust and you have to know your spouse will support you in any problem that may arise. If you cannot do this alone, a therapist can assist.

SHAME /GUILT IN SEXUAL ABUSE

In my experience, I have seen that shame is the reason why a lot of victims keep their abuse a secret. The perpetrator may knowingly, verbally abuse the victim into shame. The victim often may think he/she is to blame because of the messages the perpetrator gives the victim. Blame is also sometimes placed on others outside of the victim and perpetrator.

EXAMPLE:

Father talking to daughter:

"Your mother won't sleep with me anymore and love me. Won't you please? You want to show daddy you love me don't you?"

This not only puts blame on the mother, it also sets up the father as a victim, trying to get the child to feel sorry for him. The father is also subjecting the child to guilt. There is usually a combination of things used to manipulate a victim and keep them silent. Through journaling or talking to a therapist, you can evaluate these behaviors and sort through what happened.

Inappropriate conversation around a child can also be considered sexual abuse. I wasn't physically around my father much; however, he called fairly often. In person and during telephone calls, he would tell me dirty jokes and talk about his sexual experiences. He always called women "broads" and spoke about them as sexual objects.

When I was about twenty-two and I was working at a clothing store, a lady was waiting at the checkout counter for her friend who was trying on some clothing. We began a conversation and I could clearly hear through her accent that she was from Georgia. I asked her what part of Georgia she was from and, believe it or not, she was from my father's home town. I found out she knew my father when she was a junior and he was a senior at the same high school. That evening, I excitedly called my father to see if he remembered this woman. He said, "Oh yeah, I screwed her best friend on the steps of the high school one night." My energy sank and I pretended to laugh not knowing what to say.

A parent's or peers sexual activities do not need to be shared with a child. Children are so impressionable, and we must be careful to guide them in a healthy manner. Even when the child has become an adult, there are some things that may not belong in a conversation, especially when there is no regard for the child or person such as the case described above.

I do believe a parent and child can talk comfortably about sex. Each family has to decide what is appropriate and inappropriate, depending on their beliefs. For me, my family either didn't have any beliefs or held others' beliefs passed on to them. I received very mixed messages: Be sexual; however, it's not right to enjoy it.

When I was about four years old, I remember my father teaching me a little song and dance that seemed to amuse everyone except my mother. She would yell at my father and tell him to quit teaching me this routine. I didn't understand why my mother was so upset. My father seemed to get such a kick out of watching me perform this act for him. What I wasn't aware of was that my father had taught me a dirty version of "The little tea cup song." I was just delightfully singing, "I'm a little tea cup, here's my spout, turn me up and eat me out." You could imagine the embarrassment and shame I felt when I found out at an older age what my father was interested in teaching me. This was just the tip of the iceberg of what I felt. I also had a lot of anger with him for being inappropriate with me.

When I was about seventeen, he had come to visit and he came into my bedroom, apparently to wake me. I did awake, only to find my shirt unbuttoned and my breast exposed. My father was just sitting there next to me on my bed. I realized I was exposed and felt immediate embarrassment. My pajama top had never come open before and ... of all the times for it to happen. However, once I got into self-development and started uncovering other events in my life and events surrounding my siblings, I had to take a look at everything with a different perspective.

As a child, when my father did come into town, which was rare, I would usually stay at the hotel with him. It was a running joke just between us that I always kicked him a lot during the night. I never did this with anyone else. Now, I question why I felt like I had to protect myself in my sleep and why my pajama top may have been undone. Maybe I knew something might not be right.

I do not, at this time, have any conscious memories of my father out and out deliberately trying to have intercourse with me and I don't believe anything physical ever happened. However, I do remember that I was experiencing sexual abuse on many other levels from both my father and mother. I have a lot of speculation about his intent because of particular behavior and events. Also, my father blatantly tried to have intercourse with my sister.

The message is that none of these behaviors, whether verbally or physically, are appropriate under any circumstance at any time.

ALCOHOL/DRUG ABUSE

While working with my coach, I told him, "At least I was never addicted to drugs or alcohol," thinking highly of myself. In a joking voice but being serious, he said, "No, you're just addicted to unhealthy people, that's all." He was speaking about co-dependency.

For me, I developed dysfunctions other than chemical dependencies. However, I had the behaviors of chemical abusers because of my parents' and siblings' chemical dependencies. Long after mother quit drinking, it was discovered she was addicted to tranquilizers, and she spent time in a drug rehabilitation hospital at the age of sixty-two. I can recall as early as six helping my sister pour my mother's drinks. This was what was normal for me. My mother fell getting out of the tub one time while drunk. I can still remember saying, "She's drunk again." I got into a lot of trouble for having said it. I really stress: do not underestimate the knowledge and awareness of a child. They are very intelligent and pick up things quickly. At age seven I already had an ulcer because of the stress I was under around my family and the circumstances in which we lived. I trotted off to school with my lunch bottle of antacids and baby food. I already had a lot of fear that I would have to work through at a later time.

Even though I never had a drug or alcohol addiction, I was exposed to it for a large portion of my life. My mother used to take me to the lounge at the hotel where she worked. She would have her afternoon cocktails while I proudly ordered a "kiddie cocktail." Understand, I was about five years old! It's surely a miracle I've never had a drinking problem. I recall a time during cold weather that my sister and I had to wait outside of a bar in the snow, while my mother went in to get a new bottle. Again, I was about five and my sister about eleven. We were left unattended in the cold. I now look back and sometimes think how I'm lucky to be alive.

When individuals are abusing drugs and alcohol, it also affects the loved ones around them. I have seen abusers think that they can cover up what they are doing. We all have a natural instinct within us that tells us when things are not okay. Drug and alcohol abuse may be covered up for a while; however, it will catch up to the user.

Alcohol abuse can stem from other abuses. If you were physically beaten or molested as a child, those are not nice memories. As an adult, if you have not worked through dysfunctional behaviors, those memories may haunt you. Alcohol seems to be a choice for a lot of people who want to forget. They may not think long-term about the effects. They only want to forget about it, right now!

My experience is that chemical abuse eventually catches up to a person. It usually catches up to individuals physically, emotionally, in relationships, and on the job. I feel like most alcoholics have co-dependent traits, however, are mostly counter-dependent in behavior. A counter-dependent is a person who uses others or tries to get their needs taken care of by someone else. These individuals usually have someone around them doing things for them and cleaning up after them. The co-dependents who take care of these individuals do things such as bringing in the money and lying to employers or friends for their behavior.

If you think you may have a problem with drugs or alcohol, now is the time to get help. The issues you are trying to hide from will not go away without facing them. We are all born with an instinct to survive; however, I feel we all have it in us to do more than just survive. We all have the potential within us to live life fully and happily.

RELIGIOUS ABUSE

I remember as a child telling my friend my belief about God. I told her we were merely puppets of God and that everything we did and said was how God planned it. With this kind of thinking, how much more controlling can you get than at the hands of God? As a child, I definitely received strong negative messages about God. It's no surprise why I didn't grow up embracing God.

My beliefs came from my mother. As a child, my mother experienced a lot of religious abuse, including her pastor making a sexual advance to her. Her own mother was a religious fanatic. My grandmother had started entering my mother in talent contests at the ripe age of three. My mother won the contests almost every week. She often brought home more money through her winnings than her father would earn in the same week.

All of a sudden my grandmother "found" religion and decided these talent shows were the way of the devil. My grandmother took all of my mother's talent show awards, pictures, and costumes and put them in a pile in the yard. She made my mother watch as she burned everything. My grandmother would also take my mother down to the local jail against her will and they would sing hymns to the inmates. All of these experiences would ensure that we children would not have a healthy sense of spirituality. I learned that if you needed God, you were weak.

Because of this message, I watched my sister go in and out of several religions, one of them being Buddhism. A friend of hers was Buddhist and helped my sister get clean from being a cocaine addict. He had helped her get clean and soon after, she became Buddhist. She went from spending money on drugs to donating a lot of her money to the temple. It looked like she was jumping out of one frying pan into another. Her behavior still seemed addictive in nature and not healthy.

Being that I was brought up to have negative beliefs about God, there was a time when I had made up my mind that I would never believe in God. I had only experienced the "hell-damnation" or the "rose-colored glasses" aspects of God. Fortunately, after much self-study and discovery I had a spiritual awakening, and I learned a safe way to develop my belief in God. Now I have a very healthy relationship with Him.

There is a religious spirit that is not healthy. It often harbors fear and judgment. Spirituality on the other hand and a good relationship with God is healthy. It is my experience that you need God on board to really work your way through all of your issues.

EATING DISORDERS

Food is to nourish our bodies. Food can be just as destructive as alcohol or drugs. I've known people to abuse their bodies by gorging and purging – sending the body into complete confusion. We say we want to look good and then treat ourselves so badly. When we eat too much, and the wrong things, it seems our bodies are overloaded with waste it can't get rid of fast enough.

Plaque builds in the arteries from too much fat. Our adrenal glands burn out from too much sugar consumption and the liver is eaten away by alcohol. These are just a few of the thousands of things that can do us harm, when we abuse our bodies. This is on top of our bodies naturally growing older and developing complications. Your body deserves good nutrition, just as you deserve to be treated well. Listen to what your body tells you.

No one wants to think or feel that their parents would tell them wrong. You've probably heard the phrase "stuff yourself" when someone was talking about food. Some individuals with eating disorders stuff themselves with food, covering their feelings to avoid people and pain. It is my experience that these individuals stuff their feelings and aren't able to express themselves. I've seen other individuals starve themselves for attention and love. Eating disorders can work both ways and definitely need to be treated by a doctor.

Growing up around my house was like being in a chocolate factory. It was always full of chocolate and sweets. I did not realize until much later, what an addiction I had to chocolate and sugar. Eating was a celebration of everything. If you have a special occasion, eat. If you were sad, eat. If you were angry, eat. Chocolate in our family was used as a reward. I still find it hard to let a day go by without a "treat."

I watched my sister become anorexic/bulimic. She danced with a ballet company where no one thought they were thin enough. I've never seen anybody who could put away as much food as my sister. It was an obsession. She would sit at the table and eat her food and then promptly go to the bathroom where she proceeded to throw it up.

I remember times when we had nothing left in the house to eat. My mother didn't enjoy cooking any longer and we generally fended for ourselves with the exception of a few groceries bought each week to make our own meals. When there was nothing left in the house to eat, my sister would start getting creative. One time she mixed cereal with pancake syrup and ate it with a spoon off of a plate. We laughed at her thinking it was funny that she could put away so much food. I had no concept that what she was doing was dysfunctional. This was normal, right?

Food addiction was common in our family. Manic depression ran on my mother's side and most of the women were heavy. Food became a joy of life for a lot of my family members, as well as a security blanket for depression. "You're going to die somehow, eventually," would be their response, "Might as well die enjoying it."

I have noticed that survivors of sexual abuse commonly abuse food in order to make themselves less desirable to their offender. The belief seems to be that they can hide behind the weight and no one will see them so they are less likely to be victims. This behavior also seems to be common in individuals who have difficulty with intimacy in any relationship. Food will occupy these individuals' minds, keeping them from allowing themselves to get close to anyone. It is likely that most of these individuals have not had a healthy relationship and as an adult, makes it difficult to trust others.

In today's society, we are dealing with an increased pressure from media advertising that says "thin is in." Every billboard, magazine, and model we see is rail thin. Then we are bombarded with advertisements for diet products and centers that are popping up everywhere. The important thing is keeping a perspective on situations and everything in moderation.

Food is to keep us alive, and even though food can be enjoyable, using it as a "treat" can be an unhealthy behavior. Children can get the wrong message through this behavior. If food isn't offered to them when they are having positive behaviors, they might think something is wrong. Reward children with praise. The time to eat is when you are hungry. As adults, this behavior is hard to combat. The food used as "treats" becomes a daily habit. We also live in a society where socializing with friends usually has something to do with eating. As adults, reward yourself through positive affirmations.

SOCIETY'S HAND IN THE ABUSE

It is bad enough that we have experienced abusive situations growing up in our houses without society dealing us a dirty hand. In today's society, we are given messages that men don't cry, women are sexual objects, sexual harassment is okay, rape and violence is tolerated, along with the increasing problems of racial tension; and the list goes on. These messages are pounded daily into our head through radio, TV ads, magazines, music, movies and unfortunately, our judicial system, which lets people go when they've committed serious crimes. These are not issues that seem to be going away. They seem to be boiling and ready to explode. We cannot restrict our media, however, we need to be accountable and hold them accountable for what messages are influencing our society that perpetuates the dysfunction.

If a child is sexually abused at home and then goes to school where they are sexually taunted by a classmate and no one stops the behavior when they hear a cry for help, what message does this send? Obviously, the child will feel this is expected behavior and something they will have to learn to live with. Why, in some cases, are teachers, principals, and other authority figures afraid to jump in and stop this offensive behavior? These messages feed the behavior of keeping secrets and being silent. Also, it seems like individuals don't want to be held account-able.

Changing the behavior needs to start in the home. Close your eyes for a few moments and imagine each and every person coming from a loving, healthy family. Imagine the love between people instead of hate. Isn't it a wonderful image? And why couldn't it be like that if we all took our part in the picture?

On my sixth birthday, I had my entire classroom over for a birth-day party. It was one of the rare times my father was home. One of my friends from school who was at the party was a black boy. I liked him very much. He was always polite, quiet, and friendly. I heard my father yelling at my mother, asking her why this black child was in our house. I was very hurt. I didn't understand what was wrong with my friend. Fortunately, my father did not get too out-of- control and my friend was permitted to stay; however, the memory stayed with me.

I think back to that now with so much disgust. There was nothing wrong with my friend. He was a precious child of God. But "society" during that time made it wrong to have him as a friend. Thankfully, my mother raised me to treat everyone as equals. We need to celebrate all cultures, because without them, we might as well be a cloned soci-ety, which I understand medical doctors are working on diligently.

We each need to take action for universal change. One person can-not change everything; however, if each person were to do something towards change, we could make a big difference. It is not surprising that we are a nation with a lot of co-dependent people since our nation is co-dependent itself. Our government is always taking care of other countries needs before our needs are met right here. What does this tell the children?

These are just a few of the types of abuse that take place. Unfortunately, there are other types of abuse, and none of them discriminate with regard to sex, color, religion, nationality, age or any other factor. Even things that seem good for you such as religion, self-development, and recovery, can become addictive if not used in moderation. At the end of the day, it doesn't matter the type of abuse, what I have found is that the feelings experienced are the same for these individuals. Feelings like low-self worth, low value, doesn't fit in, shame, etc...

I've known individuals who have gotten out of one addiction only to find something good, and then become addicted to it. It seems like individuals can't get enough of a good thing; however, when they start sacrificing other parts of their life, such as sleep, health, or means of making a living, they are replacing one vice for another. The difference is that it is easier for someone to justify their obsession because it is supposed to be an area of self-restoration. You can talk your talk or walk your talk.

By now you will have a good idea how beliefs feed into setting good boundaries. All of the behaviors we have covered are important to inventory to make sure we are functioning healthy in each area. You may find other behavioral areas than the ones I have listed. When we understand our behaviors while having good beliefs on board, we can then start becoming successful with having balance in our lives. This ultimately will give us peace. Peace is the ultimate gift I wish for you to achieve.

We have covered a lot under the boundaries section. Let's recap your action steps from Chapter 2-Boundaries so that you have a full understanding of what you will need to accomplish. Use the provided checklist below.

_____ Complete a "Tree" for EACH negative belief

_____ Complete the Boundaries Inventory Graph

_____ Identify and fill out how you do not set boundaries

_____ Identify and fill out how you set too many boundaries

_____ Write how you don't set boundaries and what you are giving away because of it. Make yourself a "charm" bracelet or art project that best represents this activity.

_____ Complete all the questions throughout each section of Chapter 2.

Chapter 3

Balance

Don't worry about anything; instead, pray about everything.
Tell God what you need, and thank him for all he has done.
Then you will experience Gods' peace, which exceeds anything
we can understand. His peace will guard your hearts and
minds as you live in Christ Jesus. And now, dear brothers and
sisters, one final thing. Fix your thoughts on what is true, and
honorable, and right, and pure, and lovely, and admirable.
Think about things that are excellent and worthy of praise.
Keep putting into practice all you learned and received
from me-everything you heard from me and saw me doing.
Then the God of peace will be with you. (Phil. 4: 6-9)

Balance sounds so wonderful, doesn't it? As I have mentioned previously, it is difficult to find balance without first changing your beliefs, as well as learning how to set boundaries. You might find that this chapter is not quite as long as the last two. The reason is because most of the difficult work is within our mind's beliefs and then our behaviors. Once we have those functioning healthy then it is much easier to be in balance. Not to say that there won't be times when you will get off balance, but you will have an easier time getting things back in control because you have self-respect.

I can now say that through all of the self-development work I have done, I am very much at peace, which looks like having balance in my life. But of course, like others, life sometimes gets hectic and we have to check in and figure out why we are letting things take over again. Balance is about constantly checking in with ourselves to make sure we stay in balance.

The good news is that we have completed the really hard part! YEA! Now to implement more organization and boundaries into what you have learned, this chapter is going to give you some practical ways of setting up your life in order to have more balance, success and peace.

You have gained many tools on changing your mindset, as well as tools to assist you in setting boundaries in your life. Now it is time to grab some tools that will further those things along. You will find that these are practical tools. One of the things that my husband and I do is to sit down every Sunday night and we spend 5-10 minutes reviewing our goals. It keeps us in check with our future, our communication and it just simply connects us. I believe, to be successful in life and to have peace that we need to be in constant check with ourselves. If you feel like you need an accountability partner, work with your spouse, a friend, mentor or coach. You need to stay on track with your goals in order to achieve the things you desire. You will find in this chapter exercises and tools to assist you in doing this.

PRIORITIES

Priorities are the first step that we need to look at setting. One of the reasons our life has been out of balance, as well as dysfunctional, is because we do not have a good understanding of how to set priorities. We may say that our health is the most important priority in our life, but if you stop by the donut shop every morning on your way to work you are actually making being unhealthy your first priority. Or, if you say your family is your most important priority but you work 70 hours a week and don't spend much time with them, you are showing them with your behavior the opposite is true. So in order to begin ACTING on our priorities, we have to know what is most important to us.

Take a look at the list of priorities that follows. These are all priority areas. Read over them and if there is one you want to add or delete you may do so. You want to be able to identify your top five priorities. These will be your most important things to work on that you feel need attention in your life. Priorities 6-10 are ones that may not be as important and may raise up in the ranks as you complete your top five priorities.

If you have an area in your life that is working just fine, rank it low or do not rank it at all. Things that are functioning on auto-pilot are usually working just fine. Do not let guilt make you write something down. For instance, for many of us we know that God comes first, family and then us. This is our belief system which is different from our priorities. If you go to church frequently, know the bible well and have a great relationship with God, well, your "spiritual priorities" may be on autopilot and may not even need to be listed. You KNOW that God comes first, but if that is already happening, then no need to make it a "focused" priority. Focused priorities are things that really NEED more work or effort. Let's get started:

Work/Career

Recreation/Relaxation

Spirituality

Personal Development

Friends

Relatives

Qualifications/Education

Family

Finances

Health

Dreams

Fun

Me-time

Diet

Love/Romance

Exercise

Partner/Relationship

Children

Home Environment

Passions

Travel

5 Top Priorities

1) _____

2) _____

3) _____

4) _____

5) _____

Priorities 6-10

6) _____

7) _____

8) _____

9) _____

10 _____

Keeping hold of your priorities can be tricky if you have not gotten a hold of your internal beliefs and have begun setting boundaries. Remember, that when you stay true to your priorities you are not only honoring yourself, you are respecting yourself.

Respect is something that is easily given away when we don't have good beliefs and boundaries. When we begin setting priorities and keeping them, we begin to show ourselves respect. Respect is something that if you grew up in a dysfunctional family, you may not have learned how to do appropriately whether it is with yourself or others. Each time you work outside of your priorities, you know you are doing wrong and this infiltrates the self-esteem, often bringing those negative thoughts and feelings back.

We do not want to keep perpetuating the same behavior. This not only keeps us in our low-self worth but it destroys hopes of being successful. It also helps ensure that if you choose to have children, you will likely pass these not so nice skills on to them. Respect is about making yourself first. Respect is about making yourself important. Respect is about making yourself valuable! And, you ARE valuable! Now, act like it!

GOALS

Now that you know your priorities, it is time to begin setting goals. It is difficult to set them without knowing your priorities. Setting goals is not just writing down on a piece of paper that you want a big house, expensive car and the perfect spouse. Goals are about identifying what it is that you want in life and then mapping out a plan to get there. If we don't identify the integral steps we need to take, it will be next to impossible to obtain those things.

Goals can be material things, as well as feelings or a state of being. For instance, it can be to obtain a car or peace in your life. It is completely up to you what you desire. We need to write goals in all areas of our lives, not just one, or we once again become unbalanced. In my working with people, I have found that there are a series of important categories in which to write goals. Take a look at these categories below and make a check mark next to the ones that are pertinent in your life.

_____Career/Job

_____Finance

_____Romantic Relationship

_____Housing

_____Organization

_____Health/Fitness

_____Family

_____Children

_____Spiritual

_____Social Life

_____Education

_____Vacation/Relaxation

One of the things I have learned over the years is that to achieve a goal there must be an intense desire. You really have to want whatever it is that you are trying to achieve. Otherwise you will find yourself sabotaging your success. I truly believe that achieving goals is 10% what you do and 90% is sheer persistence.

An important thing when writing goals is to determine whether it is a need or a want. Needs of course must be taken care of before wants. Also, make darn sure that you really want that goal. Be careful what you ask for. One thing that I suggest to clients who are looking to get into a new career field is what I call, "Try it before you buy it." In other words, meet with someone doing that job first and interview them. Find 3-5 people in that career field and invite them to lunch and have a list of questions. Even see if some of them would allow you to come follow them around the work environment for a day, two days or even a week.

When I was a Corporate Trainer everybody thought that it was such a cool and glamorous job because you got to stand up in front of an audience and be the speaker. I would tell individuals that it was not quite like that but they often didn't believe me. I knew a couple of people who left their jobs and took a training job, only to discover what a challenging position it could be. Instead of jumping out before looking, why don't you peek first? We can do the same with some of our goals.

Once you establish that, yes, you want that goal; it is time for planning and development. When we have that in order, then we have to be willing to take action. Yes, I said WILLING! Goals aren't always easy to achieve. We have to be willing to put some hard work into them or they may never come to fruition. Ask yourself, have you had a goal but failed to achieve it? Why? This is an important question to ask. We have to get all of the "stuff" out of the way so we can achieve! Whether it is an old negative belief that we are undeserving or something physical holding us back, we have to figure those things out and change them! And think to yourself, once obtained, how will reaching my goal change my life? That can often keep us focused.

If you find that you have difficulty staying on task with your goals, gather assistance and resources to help you. Whether it is your spouse, mentor, coach, friend or someone else, it is important to have that accountability. Another great tool is to visualize your goals as if you have already reached them. When you are visualizing, sense what feelings you are going to have when that happens. Is it joy, security, fun? One great way of doing this is to create a vision board which I will cover later in this chapter.

In order to be successful with your goals you have to write them down. You need to make them measurable, specific and challenging, yet obtainable and realistic. Also, it is very important to set a goal date. Without that date, you may not stay focused. When working with my clients on their goals, I have them pull out their calendars, whether paper or a calendar on their phone. As we are working on goals, I have them go ahead and schedule the task in their calendar with a pop-up reminder (for cell phone/PDA users) so they can stay focused.

Let's get started on how this will look. Create a goal sheet for each category that you have check marked above. In your journal or paper pad, create each one of these pages now. Use the example provided:

Goal Category:
Specific Goal:

Long (6months or longer)

-
-
-
-

Medium (Monthly/Bi-monthly-1-6 months)

-
-
-
-

Short (Daily/Weekly)

-
-
-
-

Here is an example of how to fill one out:

Goal Category: Health & Fitness
Specific Goal: Lose 30 lbs

Long (6months or longer)

- Yearly physical with doctor
- Walk a 5k in two years
- Begin training for 5K June 1st

Medium (Monthly/Bi-monthly-1-6 months)

- Schedule doctors' appt to discuss weight - by April 30
- Lose 6 lbs by March 30th
- Lose 6 lbs by April 30th
- Lose 6 lbs by May 30th
- Lose 8 lbs by June 30th
- Lose 4 lbs by July 30th

Short (Daily/Weekly)

- Eat 1,200 calories a day
- Drink 8 glasses of water a day
- Get 7-8 hours sleep nightly
- Weigh in on Fridays at 7am
- Meal planning: Saturdays 10am
- Grocery Shopping: Saturdays 1pm
- Pre-cook weekly meals: Sundays 1-4pm
- Lose 1-2 lbs a week
- Work out 3X week: Mondays, Wednesdays, Fridays 6am
- Walk 2X weekly: Saturdays & Tuesdays

As you can see in the example above, write out dates if you can. Be as specific as possible. The more you know about the goal and what needs to get done the better. Looking at this example and having your

146

calendar in front of you, you would write or type in your work outs, your weigh-in times, your shopping times, cooking times, etc.

You may have a different method than the one above. This is just the way I do it and teach it. The way you lay it out doesn't necessarily matter; what matters is that you lay it out and that you look at it frequently: frequently being daily if possible, and at least weekly. I probably review mine every several days, and then, as previously mentioned, my husband and I review them together weekly. Remember the story I told about my husband and I being individuals who sat around wishing. Not anymore! There is no time for you to waste!

JOURNALING

I have previously discussed journaling in several different ways. I want to further this discussion as it is important to your healing process. At first, if you are having difficulty expressing your emotions outwardly, journaling can assist you in that process. Journaling is keeping a daily log of your personal emotions and experiences both past and present. It helps you to sort through your past and recognize ineffective behavior that is holding you back from what you really want in the present. I know we have already touched on several ways of how to begin or use journaling as a tool, it is important enough to reiterate.

To begin a journal, purchase a small notebook or pad that you can carry with you to work or anywhere you may be for any length of time. You never know when you may be experiencing an emotion that you may need to write about. Separate your journal into two sections. One for journaling your emotions and experiences in the present and use the second section for journaling about past experiences, behaviors, and dysfunctions you can now recognize. After time and work on your journal, you will most likely recognize a pattern between your present situations and what you experienced in your past.

Example:

Past: Father tells his child that he will never amount to anything and that he is stupid.

Present: Adult child having difficulty keeping jobs and dealing with authority figures.

These are examples of the type of things that can be uncovered from the past that may be affecting the present. However, when journaling, expressing feelings about what either happened or is happening in the situation is most beneficial. If you have a difficult time uncovering or understanding feelings, don't forget I provided the feeling list on so that you can scan through them and decide if one of them applies to the way you feel.

As children of dysfunctional families, we were not able to own our feelings, and so we may not really understand them. To help in this process, designate a third section in your journal. Every day go down the "feeling list" and define one of the feelings each day. Look the word up in the dictionary, and write down the meaning, and then write about your experience with that feeling. You may not be able to experience the feeling on an emotional level right away. You may at first have to just experience it intellectually. I think after time and journaling you will begin to reconnect with many of those feelings and therefore will become more at peace.

I have found that self-development work is very much like putting a puzzle together. You sometimes don't even have the pieces so you have to go find them. And then, once you have them, you have to figure out how to put them together. It will mean placing things incorrectly at times and then figuring out where it goes. That is life. We have to go out and find our answers and journaling is a great way of putting those puzzle pieces of life together. Journaling tells a story and will show you patterns in your life. I find that clients who consistently journal are likely to find peace twice as fast as those who don't. Think about that!

START BEING

"Doing" can become an addiction. Some individuals may feel more worthy when they are constantly on the go, making them feel important and needed. The truth is that your body needs you just as much, and the world won't collapse if you take time out. You deserve to pay some attention to yourself. The fact is that if you do too much, eventually you may fall ill and then will have to spend time getting healthy again. Let's look at many simple and great ways you can avoid this happening and can treat yourself kindly:

- Take a hot bubble bath by candle light
- Meditate for fifteen minutes, totally clearing your mind of the day's worries: This is a good daily practice
- Take a walk in the park, bring lunch and enjoy the great outdoors
- Lay out on a blanket by a pond, lake or in the soft grass
- Grab a good fiction book and retreat to privacy
- Treat yourself to a new restaurant: order healthy.
- Go to a salon have your nails done
- Go get a massage
- Take a drive out to the country
- Go buy yourself that new outfit you have been wanting
- Take a fun class at a local community college
- Go to a movie by yourself
- Have a makeover done at a nice department store
- Take a cooking class in "healthy eating"
- Make yourself a candle light dinner and celebrate yourself
- Stay at a bed & breakfast out of town

Within your goal writing session, include a page of vacation and relaxation. Within that goal page, schedule in weekly nail appointments, bi-weekly massages or time to go to the park. I know for my husband and me, our personalities are naturally ones that are on the go. We use our goal page to keep us on track so we do not get into the rut of becoming a human doing!

When you notice you are being a human doing, it is an important time to go back and evaluate what is going on in your life at that time.

Is there something emotional going on? Is there someone pressing their opinion on you? Go back to your beliefs and make sure they are in check as well as taking a look at your boundaries. Make sure everything is functioning correctly. If you are being a human doing, I bet you will find something out of step!

SELF-WORTH REMINDER

Goal: Quick step to building self-confidence

Many individuals do not understand their good qualities and how many of them they have. Many times they dwell on the negatives believing they have nothing to offer. Try this quick, eye-opening exercise.

Tools Needed:

Pad of Post-It Notes
Pen
Timer

Get a pad of sticky notes and the pen. Set a timer for three minutes. When you start the timer, begin writing one positive thing about yourself on a sticky note. It can be a quality, character or feature. Write one per post-it note. Write as many as you can until your timer goes off. Once the three minutes are complete, add up how many sticky notes you have. When I do this with clients, sometimes they are uncomfortable. When you have grown up having negative beliefs about yourself, it is often hard to think of things. Don't give up. Do the activity and then re-do the activity in a month. See how many things you have added since that time.

You may write things like:

Nice hair
Nice person
Funny
Friendly
Loyal
Etc…

Keep the post-it notes and compare. It is amazing how this activity can shift your energy when you realize the great qualities about yourself. This is a wonderful beginning to get yourself started in the right direction.

Another Great "3-Minute Timer" Topic:

UNTYING THE TONGUE

Goal: This activity is for overcoming conversation fright or fear of speaking to others in public, not necessarily for speeches, but for those individuals who even have a hard time starting or carrying on a personal conversation.

Needed Tools:

Timer
Mirror
List of topics

Make a list of topics that you can pick from. Set your timer for three minutes. When the timer starts, begin talking about a subject. The first time you do this activity start with a topic that you enjoy and then work up to conversational topics that may not be as comfortable. These could be politics, current news topics, etc. Once the three minutes are complete, ask yourself how you felt about the exercise. Most will usually be uncomfortable the first few times, but in the long run they will be glad as they become more comfortable with spontaneous conversations and learning to voice their opinions. Be sure to praise yourself on your boldness. Repeat this activity regularly to get to the comfort level you desire!

Vision Board Creation

A vision board is an expression of yourself, what you foretell and put into intention for the future. A vision board is a collection of words and pictures that "tells" that intention. Vision Boards can include areas in: Health, Wealth, Career, Relationships, Desires, Wants, Needs, etc. …the vision is YOURS!!

Here's what you need:

Imagination
Creativity…you can ask for help!
Magazines (buy ones cheap at ½ Price Books or borrow)
Cork Board or Poster Board
Push Pins or Glue
Scissors
Marker
Blank Paper
An hour or two
The ability to have…FUN!!!

Clip pictures and/or words out of magazines that fit the desired "goals & dreams" that you have for your life. I like to use a cork board with push pins so that I can take off items when I accomplish them and add new ones. Some prefer to use poster board and glue to assemble theirs. I have even had clients paste them in an empty photo album so they can take it with them. The method doesn't matter.

Begin arranging the words and pictures to suit your eye. You want to make your vision board uplifting, inspiring and personal to what YOU want and desire, not someone else's desires. Review your vision board daily. I like to look at mine and sense the feelings I will have, as if I had already achieved those things. I even take a picture of mine on my cell phone and look at it at times when I am not at home. A vision board is a great way to stay on task with goals.

Well, we have come to the end of the book but not the journey. I want you to really grasp and understand that this is a process, one to not be rushed. Becoming a balanced and "at peace person" is something that will take time, commitment, understanding, support and a great desire for a different outcome. It is my wish for you that you make this commitment and find the respect for yourself that you deserve to have true happiness.

When I did this work it took me over two years to process through all of it. I did everything I could to change the outcome of my life. I saw a coach regularly, read books on self-development, listened to tapes, went to paid and free seminars and did a **lot** of journaling. It became like a job. It had to in order to work. But, I will say this. It has been the most fulfilling work I have ever done in my life. I would not be the person I am today without it.

God has the gift of peace FOR YOU…now, receive it!

He hath delivered my soul in peace from the
battle that was against me…(Ps 29: 11)